TO my M.
AND FRIE

MW01614381

THANK YOU

Shrapnel
The Wounds I Took to War
by
Don Kabrich
Chief Warrant Officer

GOD BLESS YOU
ALWAYS!

Rush-One-Five Publishing
St. Augustine, FL, U.S.A.

DON KABRICH
3 AUG 2021

Published by Rush-One-Five Publishing
St. Augustine, FL 32080

Printed in the United States of America

Library of Congress Control Number: 2021902743

ISBN 13: 9798731333030

The individuals portrayed in this book are real, though some names may have been changed.

Dedication

To my teammates,
Kevin Morehead and Paul Mardis

Shrapnel

The Wounds I Took to War

Prologue

Germany – October, 1984

The airport shuttle made a few final turns around the last terminal building and then drove off and out on to a runway where a Boeing 747 sat by itself, ready to receive passengers. Various military assault vehicles and tanks, painted the ubiquitous olive drab green-color of military vehicles the world over, encircled the plane. Their business-ends bristled outward, locked and loaded against any attack or hijack attempt. I felt more like a hostage than a tourist. We passed through the gauntlet of security, climbed the ramp and soon were flying to our destination. Precautions taken in the airport had been incredibly lengthy – for those days – and, as we had been checked and re-checked before boarding, the aircraft felt a little too safe.

I met Mike shortly after joining my unit. He was a few years older than me and worked in the vehicle dispatch office at the motor pool. He was from El Paso, Texas, and his family were ranchers. He was quiet, reserved, and very smart; despite these differences, we became roommates. One day we had the time and opportunity to take a little R&R, so we decided to go to Israel.

Tel Aviv, Israel: 1984

I looked out the window at the Mediterranean which faded to desert in the near-distance. It had been a relatively short flight to the Holy Land from Germany, where we were stationed. I was startled by the transformation in so short a space of time, from the ancient forests and snow-capped mountains we'd flown over only hours ago, to the parched, fatigued-colored landscape below. The plane began its descent into Tel Aviv. It was mid-October, 1984, I was 19, midway through my first tour of duty, totally unprepared for the massive culture shock that awaited.

The airplane touched down and taxied to the terminal. From what I could see, vegetation was sparse, and the earth was dry; pretty much the middle east I expected. The plane came to a stop in the middle of the runway and security vehicles surrounded us. When we stepped out of the plane onto the ramp, we got another reminder we weren't in Germany anymore; there the weather had been in the mid-50s. The wind that embraced us as we walked down the ramp was well into the 80s.

We boarded a shuttle bus and were quickly delivered to the main terminal where we were subjected to a very thorough search and interrogation. Once released by Customs, I went in search of my backpack, which I found just as it tumbled onto the conveyor belt . . . in pieces. It had been dumped out and thoroughly searched. Mike's bag, too, had been ransacked. We scooped up the debris and our sleeping bags and went in search of a flat surface where we could put everything back together.

I learned almost immediately to distinguish Arabs from Israelis, though I don't know if I can explain, since appearances within each group can vary significantly. I think it must have to do with carriage and attitude. In any event, a few Arabs loitered about. The rest were Israelis, and they looked like their faces would break if they smiled. Neither group looked warm or welcoming.

We dodged into the men's room and quickly changed into shorts, T-shirts, and walking shoes, and made our way outside. It was then that I really felt out of place. As we stepped through the doors to the airport arrival and pick-up area, I'd never felt so pasty-white and out-of-place. If we two skinny, pale Americans had entertained the notion of just blending in, we were quickly disabused; a sea of Palestinians and Arabs crowded the railing, waiting for the arrival of family and friends. If ever anything stood out like a couple of sore thumbs, it was us.

From their perspective, no doubt, we were free entertainment.

All eyes fixed on us as we made our way through the throng, which parted before us like the Red Sea before Moses. Despite the heat, the men all wore long-sleeved shirts and long pants and the women, some of them veiled, wore full-length black hijabs that, to me, looked like ovens. Not that the crowd was by any means monochromatic. Bursts of color erupted from native turbans and shawls and shards of gold and silver light glanced from jewelry adorning wrists, ankles, noses, and foreheads. Everyone seemed to be very emotional and they were all talking at once. I couldn't help but feel they were talking about us. Of course they weren't.

I don't think.

At the pick-up area, car horns honked incessantly – subsequent experience has convinced me that Arabs navigate by honking. Like a cloud of starlings, they were all crying at once, simultaneously distilling enough meaningful information from the cacophony to navigate without crashing into one another.

Billows of thick black exhaust plumed from the mechanical circus and general pandemonium prevailed. The only thing yet to arrive were the traffic cops . . . or maybe they had. Still stunned, we let ourselves be funneled toward the street where, emerging from the shade of the airport overhang, we were bathed in blinding sunlight.

Overhead two fighter jets concussed the atmosphere with sonic booms. No sooner had we drawn them into focus, than they banked steeply, and were gone. I was sufficiently aware of the political situation to expect they were making runs to the Lebanese border, where Israel was engaged in intense conflict.

We could hear the beaten-pillow sounds of bombs dropping or artillery rounds exploding in the distance. Around us, no one seemed to notice. Jews and Arabs alike – all were busy living their everyday lives – shopping, gossiping, laughing, pushing babies in strollers, forever gesticulating – and all the while jets performed their deadly dance in the skies above.

The dichotomy was jarring but par for the course in this tiny, crowded strip of land claimed as a birthright by competing factions with conflicting beliefs and smoldering passions, time out of mind. Here, vengeance is the main commodity, and everybody trades in it. You never know when a chance word, an ill-timed look might ignite a storm of violence. That fact, I decided, was what made the whole absurd theater somehow less incongruous.

I looked to the east. The distant hills and valleys looked

much as I expected. I knew they echoed with a chorus of ancient stories and history kept in suspension for tens of thousands of years. I was only peripherally aware of those stories or that history at the time.

Little did I know how deeply those ancient echoes would traverse the years to affect my life.

The streets, buildings, and landmarks added further emphasis to the cultural divide. Modern Israeli buildings stood like well-ordered islands amid a sea of unfinished Arab structures of cinder block and stucco, topped with corrugated metal.

The Israeli homes were ringed by carefully-tended lawns, gardens, and orchards. Most of the Arab homes were landscaped with dirt, rocks, dust, and discarded plastic bags.

The contrast was stark, but it can't have been attributable to poverty; many of the Arab houses had new Land Rovers or Mercedes in the drive, and from the rooftops sprouted a forest of satellite dishes busily harvesting the wind for perverse, perverted, and roundly condemned western entertainment.

The streets of Tel Aviv were crowded with traffic, stop lights and corner markets; a busy clump of the 20th Century set against the backdrop of the Holy Land. Mike and I hailed a taxi and were taken to the coast. There, the beach was long and Mediterranean in appearance. It could easily be the coast of Spain or Italy. As was the case in their European counterparts, a pedestrian walkway paralleled the beach and its length was dotted with shops, cafes, restaurants, and lifeguard towers thirty feet high. As it grew late and the sun set, the beach became more deserted. For a while we just stood with our feet in the sand, watching the last wash of light slip into the horizon.

Before long, it donned on us that we were without a place to camp and decided that a lifeguard tower was as good a place as any to spend the night. Neither of us had much money, and the little we *did* have needed to last for thirty days. As it got dark, we climbed a nearby tower and spread our sleeping bags across the floor. The moon rose giving light to our impromptu shelter. Mike stood at the railing looking out. I lay in my sleeping bag listening to music on my headset.

At first, I felt peaceful, happy, and excited about where we were. I happened to be looking at Mike's silhouette standing at the railing. Suddenly, he assumed a defensive posture. He started backing up. Just then I saw the dark silhouette of a man coming up the steps. He was pointing an assault rifle at Mike who put his hands up. I watched the man and Mike exchanging words to the accompaniment of the music blaring in my headphones.

The man thrust his weapon at Mike. Instinctively, I sat up and reached to turn off the music. The sudden movement caught the intruders attention, and he swung his weapon at me. I shut off the music. "American! American!" I said. It had been a reflex, and could have been the absolute wrong thing to say. The gun barrel swung again to Mike who was apologizing even as the man – identified by the insignia on his uniform as an Israeli soldier – was demanding: "Who are you? What are you doing here?"

From our mumbled replies, he apparently deduced we weren't a threat to the nation. His aggression subsided and was replaced by annoyance. He clicked the safety on his weapon and lowered it. He seemed amused that two Americans were camping in a lifeguard tower. He explained that he'd been on patrol when he saw our movement. Logically, he assumed the worst: terrorists not tourists. "This is a dangerous place," he said, and went on to explain that, while the day belonged to civilians, and law and order was maintained by police and the army, night was the province of enemy infiltrators.

"You are fortunate," he said. "In the present climate, those of us on patrol are more apt to shoot first and ask questions later." Apparently they didn't, as a rule, take into account clueless Americans on holiday. "When I saw you move in the shadows, my training is to assume you were reaching for a weapon. Why you are standing here alive is – a miracle."

He said he'd let us stay there for the night and would keep an eye on us from time-to-time, but since there were those in the night who might just as well like to kill us, the decision to stay – and its consequences – were on our head. "I'll check from time to time to see if you're still alive," he said, as he descended the ladder shaking his head. We said 'good-bye'. He said, 'Crazy.'

We spent the night trying to sort out who did what wrong, and what we probably should have done. We also started seriously considering our safety. Israel was already proving more dangerous than the brochures stated. Even though we had learned an important lesson, it had not changed the fact that we did not have enough money to travel as safely as we would like.

The next day, we hitched rides to Jerusalem which came into view when we crested the surrounding hills. The city was crowned by the golden Dome of the Rock which, I knew, overlooked the Old City. As the sun set, I heard the call to prayer echo from all directions.

Jericho lay somewhere to the east, on the road to the Dead Sea.

I was not a Christian then. I didn't know much about the religion into which I'd been born, or the Judaism that had given it birth. My time in Israel was, therefore, just an experience to check off my bucket list, no different than a trip to Machu Pichu or the Matterhorn. I had no notion of the spiritual weight of where I was and its significance to my soul.

It would be years, yet, until the day I'd meet a Stranger who had walked that land with a simple message that would change the world – and my life – forever.

Chapter One

Shrapnel. Where to begin? With my earliest memory, dredged up from a million miles and what seems like many lifetimes ago. I'm two or three and in a camper trailer on a beach somewhere in northern California. It's most likely Pismo Beach. I'm sitting at a small wooden table bench across from my parents with a small cake in front of me. It's white with candles on it. Outside it's foggy and cold. I don't like the pointy birthday hat they put on my head, other than that, the memory brings no emotion with it. It's just something I recall, in sharp contrast to those memories yet to be made that these pages will reveal. It's a place to start.

It was the late 1960's and everything was "far-out." People wore weird clothes in shades of green and orange. Carpets were long and creepy and seemed to crawl with a life of their own. The music was eerie and strange. It was the era of the Age of Aquarius, the Mamas and the Papas, the Zodiac Killer, Banana Splits cartoons, black light posters, and lava lamps – the stamp of the unreal.

I grew up hearing songs about peace in a symphony of hostility. My world was confusing. We had black and white

TV's with rabbit-ear antennas. L.B.J. and Richard Nixon with their slicked back hair spoke of ending the war in Vietnam and, at the same time, images of marines fighting at the front in places like Da Nang and the DMZ were broadcast *a la carte* with our evening meals. Automatic gunfire and grenades erupted from foxholes, tearing indiscriminate holes in flesh and foliage; then scenes of men swaddled in bloody bandages being carried on stretchers to awaiting helicopters.

Meanwhile, on the streets of nearby places like San Francisco, Sacramento, and Berkeley, students and hippies were marching for peace. A dark mood set the scene for our country, for our town; for my home.

At five years old, in the middle of the night, looking out my window, I watched a motorcycle gang take revenge on a rival gang member. Suddenly, just across the street, a swarm of leather and denim jacketed bikers had skidded to a stop and surrounded our neighbor's house. They swarmed in with bats and knives, yelling, shouting, swearing. Our archetypal, quiet, suburban neighborhood suddenly erupted in chaos. A man was dragged out. The beams from headlights and flashlights swung frantically. Sights and sounds of bloody violence echoed from white stucco and clapboard walls throughout the neighborhood. Suddenly, as quickly as they had arrived, the gang revved away, their tires showering dirt and gravel on the man bleeding on the lawn. They had beat his face and sliced his gang tattoo from his forearm.

This was my second earliest memory.

Most of my early memories are centered on my room. I never thought about it as evil, but maybe it was. I can't remember one good or happy memory related to it. As I recall, it was small, pictureless, dreary, and starkly furnished. And for some reason, no matter what time of day, darkness draped those walls like wallpaper. It was a lonely room; a place for punishment and tears.

My mother worked, so a baby sitter named Janice would watch me. She was ancient – probably twenty – and had long brown hair. She liked having her boyfriend around. When my mom was there, Janice was friendly and polite: the model of babysitterhood. But when my mother was gone her whole personality changed, revealing her as much more shadow than sunshine. She was mean-spirited and cruel. She'd often lock me out of the house just for fun. It seemed like hours I sat outside waiting, pleading and crying as the clammy dew settled on my face and pajamas. She'd laugh at me and taunt me from the open window.

Once she stopped the neighborhood bully in front of the house and made me fight him. I was five, confused and too innocent to even understand what fighting meant. I just stood there giggling. Then, with Janice's encouragement, the bully suddenly hauled off and hit me in the face. I fell stunned holding a bleeding nose while she laughed uncontrollably in the background. And then she finally allowed me to come inside so she could clean the blood off before my mother came home.

One of the last memories of my babysitter took place in that bedroom. She had sent me there as punishment. I stood for what seemed like hours staring out my window watching and waiting for my mom to come home. I quietly sobbed hoping and wishing. Janice opened the door and asked in her deadliest, sweetest voice, "Do you miss your mommy?" She came to my side, as if to comfort me. I nodded and wiped my arm across my eyes. Without warning, she slapped me hard across the face, and screamed: "She isn't coming home! Maybe never! Stop whining!" With that she turned, stomped out of the room and slammed the door. My tears flowed even harder. Why had she hit me? What had I done? What did she mean my mother might never come home?

The early 1970's seemed like a repeat of the 1960's. Not much had changed. We had moved to San Jose, a small city that rested in a dry, smoggy valley in the Bay area. It was surrounded by the brown hills to the east towards Sacramento and butted up to the south and west by the green mountains leading to Santa Cruz. The boulevards were lined with a mix of maple, palm, and oak trees. Many of the homes were ranch style and one-story Spanish types. We lived in a small corner house on Stuckey Drive just off the main boulevard. A cement-lined creek bordered by a chain link fence was just around the corner. Old orchards and fields dotted the landscape between the neighborhoods to which they were slowly surrendering. A scattering of derelict barns and chicken coops, rusting cars, trucks, and tractors sat at tired angles like tombstones to the past.

In those days, I walked to school. I don't remember much about the first grade except having a tonsil infection which effected my hearing, causing me to fall behind in class. I remember starting first grade over again and watching all my former classmates walk by on their way to second grade. My Mother tried to assure me it was no big deal, but even the seven year-olds knew better. What had I missed during those few weeks that was so fundamental to my education that it warranted that humiliation?

From that day forward, I felt defeated, a failure, forever watching from behind as my peers went on ahead. And every year, some new kid would ask me why I was older, taller and still in the younger class. I spent many hours alone, supervising myself. My mom worked a night shift of some sort and slept during the day. While she slept, I was left to my own devices. I was five or six when I stole one of her cigarettes and matches. I remember walking toward the small church at the end of the block. An orchard butted up to the back of the church. I figured that was as good a place as any to try the cigarette. I lit it, put it to my lips and puffed as I had watched my mother do a thousand times. Nothing much happened. I had lived with second-hand smoke in my lungs all my life. I kept wondering if I was going to get caught.

I looked at the church. It was an odd building, and felt abandoned. Even at that young age, though, I sensed something different about it; something about that cross on the door.

When I got home my mom was awake. Somehow, though a perpetual cloud of smoke hung in the house, she smelled *my* cigarette. She grabbed me by the face, opened my mouth to assure herself with a sniff, then slapped me. She yelled and was quite upset.

She was paying attention to me.

One day Janice took me to her church. She was as surprised that I wanted to go as I was that she asked me. I'd have gone anywhere, just to get out of the house. I don't know what kind of church it was. What I remember most vividly is that the man preaching was loud and angry and very serious about something. He was animated, sweating, and wanted people to respond to him. I didn't understand a word he was saying. I mean, I understood a lot of the words, but what he was saying made no sense to my six year-old mind. I felt like I'd entered a lecture that had begun many days before.

We'd gone there by ourselves, slipping in the back, and we left before the angry man's last echo died. We didn't talk to anyone, and no one talked to us. To this day, I don't know why she went to church, or why she asked me if I wanted to go that day. It seemed it was a private thing she did. I remember thinking that the fury of the preacher somehow seeped into her, recharging Janice with anger and meanness for another week of babysitting. She genuinely seemed to enjoy her secret abuse of me.

I wondered if she'd be a nicer person if she stopped going to that church.

One day Dad got a new job; it was exciting. He'd quit sales to become a police officer. He was training and exercising and seemed motivated. I remember feeling proud, excited by the stories he'd tell of his experiences. During the day I'd ride my bike up and down the street pretending to be a traffic cop. I wrote down the street intersections and so on. It took me an hour to write those few words but it was part of the job. It wasn't long before the home got quieter and lonelier with mom working days and dad nights. I was left to make my own way through the days.

Mom was picking me up from a neighbor's house after school. I'm not sure exactly what triggered it, but Dad started drinking. He'd tell me scary, true-life horror stories about the people he tracked down on the dark streets: burglars, murderers, crazy people. He held nothing back. His vivid descriptions took on a life of their own in my fevered imagination. I was seven, and familiar with Evil.

For some reason my mom kept me in my room as much as possible. It was not a comforting place; there were no childhood decorations, not much to play with, and when the door closed, it was pitch dark. I had a hard time falling asleep in that much dark. And one particular night while it was thundering, I wandered to my parent's room and stared at the dark figures sleeping peacefully. Sometimes I would just sit there in the shadows, watching. Somehow it made me feel I belonged. A couple of times I ventured to lie on the edge of their bed, careful not to wake them.

But on one particular night, lying in my room, I thought I heard a strange noise in the house. With my dad's descriptions of burglars ever-fresh in my head, that's what I imagined it was. I thought I saw a dark figure enter my room. My eyes were playing tricks on me in the darkness but I was scared. I cried and yelled out anyway.

All of a sudden, another dark figure came through the door. This time more real. It was my father, enraged at my crying. He started to slap and hit me, yelling at me to be quiet. I was terrified.

As quickly as he had come in, he left, slamming the door behind him. I was left to come to terms with the fact that it wasn't some strange intruder I had to fear, it was my dad. That night, he became my nightmare. I sobbed under my covers in the dark. This was my last memory of that room.

Soon we were moved again.

I brought my bike and, with my ever-present notepad, pretended to be a policeman in our new neighborhood. On a fresh page, I wrote down our street name and the number of the house. Dad brought with him his ever-increasing anger. Mom brought her same busy self.

Just before the move, my parents tried to drive home drunk from a party and slammed into a parked car. They went to the hospital leaving me home alone, not knowing why they hadn't returned, or where they were. This heightened my normal sense of abandonment and fear. I was eight years old.

My parents sometimes went to church on Christmas or Easter. It wasn't like my babysitter's church. No one shouted from the podium. There were priests in black robes with stiff white collars. Maybe the collars scratched, and that's what made them sad. It was contagious. Their sadness was reflected on the faces of the people; even the statues looked sad – but none as sad as the man on the cross in the window.

The sound of creaking bones and squeaky kneeling benches punctuated the service, which was in Latin. A foreign language in a foreign world. In unison, all the sad people repeated words they read from papers in their hands. My overall impression, still vivid after all these years, was of a cold, strange, and eerie place that echoed with the ab-

sence of a loving God – whoever He was. Even when I went to First Communion I did not feel like I was doing anything real or necessary. I was looking at Bible storybooks with colored pictures and still feeling uncomfortable around the priests in their black robes and the nuns in their black habits, over-sized crucifixes dangling from their necks or swinging in their hands. I can't remember any of these experiences as evidence for the existence of God. I didn't feel a deity near me. I wasn't compelled to consider good and evil or their consequences. There were no moments of clarity or conviction; and certainly no feeling of God knocking on my heart, like he did in a little brochure I saw in the vestibule.

Today, I am bothered that none of these experiences ever made a spiritual impact on me. I so needed God in my life, but I didn't hear His voice in those churches. Why not? I was an innocent child with a big heart who was willing to be loved, open to a relationship with God. I wish I could have had the epiphany that I know so many other young children had. Why, if church was God's house, did I never find him home?

To the contrary, it seemed a perverse rule during those early years that the nicer and warmer I tried to be, the more abuse I got. At every turn in my young life I was being hit, abandoned, taken advantage of, fearing for my life, being punished in ways too hurtful to detail. I was never loved, I was tolerated – only just. Respect was demanded of me, but never shown me. In fact, as soon as I was able to understand, it was made clear to me that I was a financial and personal burden. Back then this was all I knew. I have since learned that it is not normal to be treated the way I was.

But God never came to my rescue. Jesus never visited me. I was surrounded by churches and church-going people but never heard a word about God's love and salvation in

Christ. I never heard a conversation about the private faith of people and was never asked to accept Jesus into my heart. In the mindscape of my young brain imaginary friends rescued me.

I so wish Jesus had visited me back in all those lonely, quiet hours spent by myself. I did not experience a miracle of divine intervention. God didn't send a loving Christian along to invite me to youth group, or to place a Bible in my hand. I wasn't transformed by a TV evangelist I just happened to see as I flipped through the channels. Years later, I'd heard of these things happening, but they never happened to me. How different my journey might have been if they had.

Chapter Two

The move took us from the small little house on Stuckey Drive to the newer more modern neighborhoods in the Almaden Hills. By then my dad had been a San Jose police officer for a few years, and my mother had trained to become a deputy sheriff for Santa Clara County. She would work in the women's jail. Financially life was better. The increased income was affording us more comfort and security. We had a two-story house with a swimming pool and large backyard overlooking the city from the end of a cul de sac. The rolling hills and new construction were a significant change from what I was used to. The homes were nestled up against the mountains leading to Santa Cruz and Salinas. The neighborhood looked much like the one in the movie *E.T.*, a perfect place for kids to explore and embark on adventures.

In the 1970s, boys and their bikes were intimately connected. We'd gather in the circular drive early in the morning and not come home for hours . . . often until it got dark. It wasn't uncommon to hear mothers calling out to their children when it was getting late. Sometimes you would hear them whistle or even honk horns. I spent many hours playing and exploring in the nearby trees, hills, and miles of neighborhood streets. My friends and I would make ramps for our bikes and skateboards. We'd make forts and play hide and seek.

In those days, TV didn't monopolize children's time the way iPhones and computers do today. There were only a few channels, and no remote control. Of course there were a few shows we set our internal clocks for, but not many. Besides, parents didn't like their kids hanging around inside the house. "Go outside and don't come home 'til lunch!" was a common refrain. That's one command we had no problem following. Outside we'd go and there our imaginations would take hold.

Childhood games and fantasy occurred as they should. Some of my best, albeit mixed, childhood memories happened there. I enjoyed swimming, being a pitcher in Little League, and being a goalie for the "Avalanchers" soccer team. I jumped rows of garbage cans on my bike and ran my skateboard fast down the steep streets and hills around my neighborhood. Like most kids, I was highly active, learning what life had to teach me, good or bad, without the guidance – apart from instinct – to really know the difference.

One day when my friends and I were playing outside the house, my dad drove up in his black and white police car with his partner. I thought he looked so cool. His black uniform, shiny black boots, black police belt, and gun all seemed out of place in those suburban surroundings. His expression, accented by his slicked back black hair and mustache, was always intense. He was all business.

The police radio was squawking in the background as he opened the trunk to show off his arsenal of weapons. His partner Gill was easy-going, contrasting sharply with Dad who wore a chip on his shoulder like a second badge. His name was Bob, but his buddies in the Department called him "Fruitcake." In retrospect, I suppose that's because, at five foot seven, Dad always felt that he had to prove himself, and so was always doing something to shock his comrades.

In those days, the police sort of followed their own set of rules; it actually seemed like they had to make them up as they went along; like it was the wild, wild west. Everything was reduced to black and white; good guys and bad guys, and the police were the good guys, even during bad days. They ruled the streets, arrested whomever they needed, and intimidated as necessary. At night when the shift was over they'd gather in the nearby park and drink confiscated beer and shoot out lights. They would leave the scene blaring *Apocalypse Now* music from their squad cars.

Fruitcake had a crazy, hard-charging reputation. One night there was a problem at an apartment complex on a bad side of town and several police officers were on the scene trying to calm things down with diplomacy and whatnot. Then Bob showed up. One of the officers saw him pull up and get out of his squad car and said, "Uh oh. Fruitcake's here." Without hesitating, my dad walked back to his trunk, pulled out an M-16 assault rifle, and strafed the upper level of the apartment complex. Everyone dove for cover, and complete silence followed. Fruitcake had quickly and surgically rectified the situation. Of course it was beyond right or acceptable, but cops like Bob got away with it and were actually encouraged. At one point he threatened to kill every last one of the residents of the apartment complex if they didn't cease. No one could say it wasn't an effective tactic in a brutal, primitive kind of way.

On another occasion Fruitcake and his rookie partner were called to a possible suicide/homicide. He had just picked up a cup of coffee and a powdered doughnut. He brought them with him. As he walked through the crime scene with his partner in tow, finding the deceased with their throat cut lying bloody and naked in the bath tub, he simply got down next to him sipping his coffee and eating his doughnut. Careful not to get any powdered sugar on his uniform, he reached in to feel for a pulse. Without emotion, he just said, "Yep. I think this one's gone." The rookie was mortified and said, "How can you eat a doughnut and do that?" He then went outside to throw up.

Fruitcake thought of himself as ruthless. His heroes were men like Stalin, Genghis Khan, Hannibal, and Alexander the Great. The more darkness and brutality he saw, and the more he experienced, the more it fueled him to be mean and cruel, heartless and numb. He thought that's what it meant to be tough, to be a man, and he had a badge to back him up. The only regret he mentioned some years later was seeing a gang

member on the east side of San Jose sitting shot and most likely dying. At one point the young man was leaning up against his police car. My dad didn't want him bleeding on his tire and told him to get away from it.

There was also the time he left a shotgun barrel impression on the forehead of another gang member. He pressed down so hard that it made a deep round cut on his forehead. These were just a few of the things he was willing to admit had bothered him. I shudder to think what he *didn't* tell us.

As a member of MERG (Military Emergency Response Group), better known as SWAT, he was at the leading edge of most of the action in the city. I even remember seeing his picture in the newspaper once. He was shown leaning over a fence in an alley with his shotgun resting on it, aiming at the back of an old house. Armed bank robbers were cornered, and my dad waited to shoot them down as they ran out the back. There were many more stories of the exploits of my dad's short career at the police department.

In all, he spent seven years on the force. Then one day he suddenly quit. He revealed years later it was fear of having to go through another dark room and one more doorway, where the unexpected could cost him his life that made him give up the force. The fear of the unknown and the odds of survival ever decreasing had become too much.

I did my best to lead a normal life, but my father had become increasingly more volatile and unpredictable, often drinking himself to the point of passing out. On a nightly basis after returning from play, I would come home to a tense atmosphere. Invariably he'd be drunk, stumbling around like a grenade with the pin pulled out. Everyone had to watch his or her behavior carefully so that nothing would light the fuse.

Invisibility was my best defense. I tried to do nothing that would remind my father of my existence. He'd stumble around the house, tinkering with home projects indoors and out, guzzling beer the whole time. Everything would be fine until something lit his fuse. He'd come looking for me, shouting questions at me, his springs tight in anticipation of an unsatisfactory answer, ready to pounce.

Of course, there was no right answer. Even if I had no idea what he was talking about, I'd apologize. "I didn't mean to . . ." Nothing I said would diffuse his anger. He'd press against me, pushing me back until my only response was "Don't hit me." He'd say, "Hit you? I'd never hit you." But he'd always convince himself that whatever I said was a lie, and that's just what he'd do.

It was more terrifying than painful. This crazy person who had me cornered, who suddenly struck out in rage for no apparent reason, was my dad. His attack was always quick, exact, hard, and humiliating. My instinct was to duck or run. The first few blows were to my head or stomach. And when I attempted to evade the next blow, he'd kick me as hard as possible wherever the boot could land, following up with a lunging, grabbing action.

One of three things would typically happen then, either he'd exhaust his fury on me, or I'd escape, or he'd just give up. Afterward, to survive, I would hide for hours from this man who hurt me, who lied to me, who seemed to hate me at times and wanted me gone.

My father.

Almost as a matter of course, I'd make it to bed after he'd passed out. Eventually, he'd call for me in a calm, reassuring voice. I'd slink back like a beaten dog who had no choice but to obey, every muscle tense and ready to flee at his slightest motion. When I felt it was safe to approach him I'd do so, talking all the while, trying to determine – by his responses – if he was trying to trick me. More often than not he was the archetypal remorseful drunk, shedding tears and begging me for forgiveness. He'd demand bear hugs and declare us best buddies. "You're my best friend, right? I love you, Son."

I was ten years old and locked in an embrace I neither understood nor wanted. If this was love, I might not survive it.

In the mornings before school, after my bowl of Cheerios, I'd run out of the house, hop on my bike and race down the cul de sac around the corner going as fast as I could. I'd meet my friend Kurt coming fast down his street from the opposite direction. At the corner, we'd link-up side by side and race three miles down the long and winding neighborhood streets, crossing from one side to the other, jumping curbs and sometimes the garbage cans in front of us.

It was the best part of the day; peddling thirty miles an hour, free as the wind, speeding, jumping, defying death and gravity all the way down to Los Alamitos Elementary School where, in perfect tandem, we'd skid to a stop in the bike racks. I knew the other kids were impressed by this performance. It was something I did well and in the brief passing glow of their respect, I was able to forget the things they made fun of me for.

These usually were the result of two physical defects, a hearing impairment and a strong lisp. I'd do everything I could to complete sentences by not using "s" sounds like Sylvester the cartoon cat. Invariably, they would come out. The kids around me would prod me to repeat whatever I'd said. And I would. And they'd laugh. In time, I became identified by that speech defect. Wherever I went everyone wanted to be entertained by me and my lisp. It was embarrassing and humiliating.

I avoided as many chance meetings as possible. The worst moments were when my teacher, Mr. Korea, would call on me to read a sentence off the blackboard. He seemed to think making me face my fears would help me overcome them. However hard I tried to stay invisible in the back, he'd call on me. He wanted me to get beyond caring about what other people thought and thereby conquer my speech impediment. As I began to read the sentence the whole class would break out in laughter. Mr. Korea didn't reprimand them. He would just wait until they stopped laughing so I could start over. Again, I tried to say the "s" words on the chalkboard. More laughter, more cutting jibes, more embarrassment.

That speech impediment went with me everywhere, calling attention to me when that's what I wanted most to avoid, betraying me to every person I met. The affliction was like a separate entity. I could almost have given it a name – like kids do with an imaginary friend. Only it was neither imaginary nor friendly. It accompanied me to third grade, fourth, fifth, sixth – all the way into my freshman year. It would be many years before I could look someone in the eye without fear of my own mouth betraying me.

Back at home my dad didn't just terrorize me physically but verbally as well. Every exchange with him seemed to include calling me an idiot, stupid, or lazy. One day I was in the kitchen with my parents when I put my hand down on a stove burner. I thought it might be warm but it was actually still very hot. I pulled my hand off and immediately noticed large blisters forming. My father just looked at me, his young, inquisitive son and said laughing, "You're an idiot." And he didn't let up for ten minutes. Meanwhile my hand needed attention.

He often drove blind drunk, and it terrified me. He was sometimes so impaired it was a miracle we never had a fatal car crash. Often we'd travel back over the mountains from Santa Cruz where my grandparents lived. It would be late in the evening. The road was narrow, steep, and windy, and the highway infamous for accidents. Mom would beg him to pull over and let her drive and he'd snap back at her – his speech slurred as if on a handful of tranquilizers – "I'm all right!" The car would swerve side-to-side, sometime dangerously close to the cliff edge. Other times, he'd snap the wheel at the last second, barely avoiding a head-on collision. I sat paralyzed and white-knuckled in the back seat of our old 1960's Volvo. I sat whispering to myself, praying to survive the death-defying drive home: forty-five minutes of terror.

Miraculously we would make it home safely into the driveway.

Arriving home, it could go either way; he'd watch TV and pass out or demand everyone watch and listen to him slur his way through one of his stories. These would be about his time in the Army, college, or police force and as he related them he chain-smoked. There were always two or more cigarette butts smoldering in ashtrays around the house. My policy was to keep quiet – interruptions could send him off on interminable tangents – until the weight of memories closed his eyes. Usually he'd pass out in his easy chair.

Chapter Three

It wasn't all bad, all the time though. I remember times we went camping, to the beach, or horseback riding without incident. My dad even played catch with me a time or two. And when I really did deserve punishment he would be nice to me instead: another perverse ingredient in the dysfunctional recipe of our relationship.

I knew how to stay busy but still managed to find trouble. Once while my father was inside GEMCO, a 1970's version of Walmart, I waited for him out in the parking lot. To pass the time I kept throwing rocks over the very tall glass "GEMCO" sign. I threw one too many. The last one went right through the middle of the sign and glass rained down around me, draping me in shards of guilt. The mess seemed disproportionate to the size of the rock. I gulped, walked inside and found my dad. After explaining, we walked out to survey the damage. Then he told me we better go tell the manager. And that's exactly what we did. Not only did I not get in trouble for the massive damage caused, but both my father and the manager were strangely fascinated, wondering how I could ever throw a rock up that high.

On another occasion, I managed to send a baseball and a basketball through the same large front window in a single day. No sooner had the glass company come to repair the window than a friend and I broke it again. Once again Dad calmly said he had done much the same thing when he was a kid. And there was the time when I removed all the insulation from the attic to make a fort. My dad just explained why the house needed the itchy pink stuff, then he compassionately rinsed me off with some cool water. There were other terrific father and son moments, but they created confusion with my dad's violent reactions to minor mistakes. Overall my childhood was a psychological mine field.

The lesson was that I could be punished furiously when I'd done nothing, and forgiven when I'd done something even *I* recognized as worthy of punishment. Where were the rules? How was I supposed to safely navigate such treacherous waters without a compass?

In 1975 American culture was pretty strange. I thought religious people were odd. All the churches looked closed off and not very inviting. The atrocities of Charles Manson and his "Family" were still fresh on everyone's mind. Adherents of Hare Krishna would prance along the sidewalks, spinning in circles, clanging cymbals and chanting the same thing over and over.

As I write this, and as much as I would like to recount a positive Christian experience, I can't. By that time I had somehow acquired a rudimentary awareness of God, and that He was supposed to be working in people's lives, in truth, the last place I wanted help from was religious people. There seemed to be a falseness and something somehow selfish in their faith, that if I didn't see things as they saw them, then salvation – even God Himself – was beyond my grasp.

I couldn't imagine such people understanding or being capable of rescuing someone like me. That, I thought, could only be accomplished by sober-minded, rational professionals with a scientific approach. Despite that, I did have a rudimentary sensation of a spiritual dimension, at least enough to blame God for my situation and feel sorry for myself that He didn't love me any more than my earthly father did. And He was just as capricious and willing to let me suffer, no matter how bad things got. I felt expendable.

The only comfort I ever found was feeling sorry for myself. I mourned my young life and quietly embraced my dad's negative opinion of me. It felt comforting to agree with the judgments made against me. I was stupid, an idiot, a wimp, and a stuttering klutz. It was easier to give up, to be defined by his low opinion of me, to surrender to the challenges that faced me, rather than conquer them.

There is a sickening, perverse kind of peace in surrender to hopelessness. You can't lose what you don't have.

After he left the police department, my dad attempted lots of jobs. He owned a water softener business and was a long-haul trucker. In between, he took jobs in security and several other odd jobs. This was when his drinking was at its worst. Many nights I'd pretend to be asleep to avoid having to deal with him. Other nights I awoke to screams and crashing furniture. I'd get up and stand alert at my door, ready to run into the night.

One morning after one of these typical night scares, I walked around to investigate. Dad was still passed out in the easy chair and my mother was upstairs in bed. Both her eyes were black and blue, almost swollen shut. I woke her up to see if she was still alive. She got up, looked in the mirror, and went into a rage of her own. Downstairs, she found Dad in his chair and started slapping and hitting him, yelling and screaming. Confused and disoriented, Dad threw his hands up to defend himself.

Another typical Saturday morning at the Kabrich house in the Almaden hills.

There were many moments like this and some even worse. After a few years we were packing up to move again. We went from an above average, middle class suburban neighborhood three hours east to Auburn in the secluded foothills of the Sierra Nevadas. I was twelve years old.

I can't remember being devastated by the decision to move. Perhaps things would be better where we were going. That wasn't to be though. A last Almaden foothills photo. A final memory of being there. We'd just gone from Egypt to the wilderness.

My nearest new neighbor was a mile away. Beyond them I knew no one. For the short year our family lived in Auburn – before packing up again to move to the Northwest

– my dad did some more useless soul searching. He talked about opening a tool rental company or getting into real estate. He did neither. Instead, he bought a small campground and trailer park. There too, my dad sloshed around getting drunk and becoming increasingly more irritable.

The dilapidated park was littered with old, rusting, single-wide trailers, work sheds, a large barn, and a country store all nestled among the dry grass and brush-like Manzanita trees found along the Bear River. It was just off the old highway that ran between Auburn and Grass Valley; the *Gold Country* foothills. I spent time swimming down the rapids, grabbing a candy bar from the store, and watching Dad kick the goat that we inherited with the campground.

The goat chewed the grass down, grazing in a circle with a rope staked to different patches. Dad would kick the goat from one extent of the rope to the other. He'd yell and scream at it as if it was guilty of something. It was probably not eating in the right direction or not going fast enough. The poor animal didn't stand a chance. The large bell around its neck would gong violently as he was being beaten trying to escape. I just sat watching from a distance hearing the thud for each time my father's boot made contact. I knew how that felt.

A dark tree line secluded the house from the rest of the world. Dad wanted isolation and didn't care if we had to suffer for it. We'd gone from a large city and a crowded suburban neighborhood to utter isolation. And from riding my bike and feats of derring-do with my friends to playing and exploring by myself on the lonely mountain range. The familiar sounds of the city gave way to the strange sounds of wildlife and the ever-groaning trees that swayed back and forth in the wind. However, I adapted. It wasn't long before I had become a mountain boy of sorts, chasing deer through the undergrowth, climbing hundreds of feet into the air, ascending the limbs of the tall pines where, swaying in the top, I'd make wolf calls at the world.

I also spent a lot of time in, on, and beside the river. Whirlpools and waterfalls were magical to me, each holding its own particular fascination. From the cliffs, I'd jump into the clear, cold waters below and slip downstream to the rapids for a short, wild ride. A mountain aqueduct zigzagged through the hills. I surrendered to its current, leaving my imagination to keep up as I plunged toward the valley below. To me, this was freedom. I wasn't lonely; all of nature was my companion. Misery may wait at the end of the day when I dragged myself home, but there in the mountains, I was free.

Every day after school I walked home. In the summer it was blistering hot, but it was even hotter in the bus. It took an hour to get to the drop-off point and then I had to hoof it four miles home. I'd start out in the valley where plowed fields predominated and climb several hundred feet to the pines. Farmhouses and corals dotted the landscape. A wooden fence ran along one side of the road, and a barbed wire fence lined the other, forming the edge of the world for a few horses and several head of cattle.

Among the horses was a pony that would always come running, clearly excited to see me. He'd whinny, and jump and stomp the earth as he darted along beside me on his side of the fence. His big eyes and shiny coat flashing in the sun. Each in our own way, we reveled in one another's company for a while until, finally, it was time for me to head home. He seemed to share my reluctance at parting but, at the same time, to understand.

When I finally reached the steep, windy stretch into the pines, the shade brought cooling, but the shadows were harbingers of night, and night brought fear. From the distance I sometimes heard the pony whinny, as if cheering me on. That gave me courage for the homestretch. I tried to embrace the pony's strong spirit as I walked around the final corner to the place that, for lack of another, was home.

The Sierra Nevada Mountains were covered in one part by dry, mixed, shrub lowlands and the other by monumental pines. From there the landscape plummeted through granite fissures and canyons eventually flattening and sprouting the bushes and tall grass of the lower elevations. To me, the mixed vegetation in the forests and hills symbolized my interior tumult. It, too, was neither one thing nor the other. I was a son but not welcome in my own family; I was a foreigner among my peers, with a home, but somehow homeless. Deep inside, though I'd never really experienced it, I knew there was a balance my life was missing; a belonging.

Out in the open fields, it was hot and dry. Rattlesnakes rattled their beads and black widow spiders scampered into the shadier sides of the sheds and outbuildings. A steady buzz of insects could be heard vibrating through the surrounding hills. I tried to explore with youthful excitement all of it. I swung on the rope that hung from the thick limb of a big oak that sat on the property. It swung me down low and deep off a ridge and, if I looked up, offered me a glimpse of snow-covered peaks. Just when I thought I had found life the way it should be, real life showed up.

Occasionally the long ride home on the bus was boring and sometimes a bit less. It always felt like I was sitting in a microwave however. On one particularly eventful day though, I brought unwanted attention to myself. The kid beside me had been happily carving designs in the seat cushion with an X-acto razor knife. We were about halfway home when, suddenly, he reached down and sliced my shoelaces. I instinctively reached down just as the kid jerked his hand up and away, slicing my middle finger one end to the other down to the bone. Immediately my hand palm pooled with blood.

I tried to control the flow with my other hand and we both called out to the driver for bandages. Back came a few Band Aides, so old they were fused to their paper wrappers. I raised my arm so the driver could see the full extent of my injury. In the rear-view mirror I saw his eyes go wide, and the bus screeched to a halt. Of course all the kids gathered 'round to see the blood. I remember one, in particular, who kept asking me if I was going to pass out, "Like they do on TV!" He was disappointed that I didn't. However, several white gauze bandages were produced and the driver wrapped them tightly around my wound.

When the bus finally pulled up to the stop everything

seemed like it was in slow motion. My dad was leaning unsteadily against his pickup truck. I knew that belligerent look, the posture. I lowered my hand. Even in his condition, though, he knew something was wrong. Perhaps he could see it on the kids' faces. I watched his disappointment mount. He just shook his head. I slowly made my way along the aisle and down the steps, where he met me. He looked at the blood-soaked bandage on my hand, then up at me, shaking his head as if I'd let him down. He reeked of alcohol but, despite his inebriation was able to feign concern for me as he walked me back to the truck.

The bus pulled away, heading back down Lone Star Road towards the highway trailing a cloud of dust and exhaust fumes. Dad and I got in the truck and the lecture began and he kept it up until, rather than taking me to the hospital or the doctor's office, we arrived home. There, he said he needed to pick up a few things. I kept saying I needed to go to the hospital and he kept saying "Yeah, we will. It looks pretty bad. But I need to get something first."

What he needed was a drink. Then another. And another. Even the sight of blood flowing down my arm was not enough to yank him out of himself, to make him put someone else's needs above his own.

Finally when he was good and drunk we headed to the hospital twenty miles away and, miraculously, we made it. Dad made a pathetic, drunken attempt to turn on the charm as the nurse took us into a treatment room. He was attempting to minimize the situation, but the nurse had to apply a solvent before she could remove the bandage. I started to tear up and winced in pain. The nurse didn't attempt to conceal her concern. "How long ago did this happen?"

Dad pretended to be shocked. He began to sob explaining he didn't realize, didn't know. "I came as quick as I could. Have to be careful on the roads, these days. Crazy drivers." The truth was, the only way we could have gotten there any earlier would be if he'd had his fill of drink before I got out of the bus, or had had the presence of mind to bring his bottle with him.

The doctor walked in. He had a quick talk with the nurse who got him up to speed on the situation. A hasty examination told him that immediate action was required, so he didn't bother to berate my father, though it was evident he'd drawn certain conclusions from his drunken condition and the state of my injury that weren't too far short of the mark.

He submerged my hand in a sterilizing solution, reopening the wound – over which blood had already crusted – in order to scrub it clean. The pain stung like nothing I'd ever experienced, and I cried out in pain. Dad cried out, too, but his tears were for himself, having been caught out in his carelessness.

Seventeen stitches later we drove home in silence. I went to my room. Dad went to pour himself a drink. That night I sat in my room questioning my worth as a human being. After all, if my own father *did not* care enough about me to rush me to the hospital when I was severely injured, why should anyone else care?

Chapter Four

Our year in the California foothills passed quickly, then Dad announced we were moving to Northwest Washington. No one protested. Too much had gone wrong where we were. In so short a time, that house had accumulated too many bad memories; you could almost smell their residue. A fresh start and a clean slate were just what was needed. Maybe a new location, a new state, would open the door to better times.

As soon as 7th grade was over we made the journey up north. The moving trucks had gone on ahead. I was glad to be leaving but would miss the pony, the whispering treetops, and the gold-flecked river, the patient companions of my solitude.

Somewhere in that solitude, I felt the first vague stirring of spiritual awareness. Some of my school mates talked about going to church with their families. Bible studies and youth group meetings were part of their lives. Often on Monday mornings they'd talk about what had happened at church the previous day.

In the life of my family, God was nowhere to be seen. I wondered why. I knew Dad was once an altar boy. He even went to a prestigious all-boy Catholic college prep school, called "Bellarmine" in San Jose, California. My mother attended a Methodist church as a girl, taking her younger brother with her to services. For a short time, she even attended Whitworth University, a Christian college, in Spokane, Washington.

Church had once been part of their lives but, I concluded, faith had no part in it. My bruises testified to that sad fact. I wondered if, like my now-former classmates, they'd ever felt they had the answers to life's questions. Somewhere they'd lost their way. Life had stolen those answers so, rather than rising to challenges, they'd surrendered to them in defeat.

That's all retrospect. At the time, I had nothing but the most nebulous concept of spiritual matters. I was taught nothing of God. I can't help but wonder how different things would have been if my parents hadn't abandoned their beliefs – or at least those things they once professed to believe.

That was not to be. Off we went to the Great Northwest and a bright shiny fool's gold promise of a better life. What we would do there, no one seemed to know exactly. By the time it became evident, it was too late.

Bellingham, Washington

There was a cool, low hanging fog stretching across the most northwestern fishing port in the lower forty-eight. The smell of seaweed and salt was perpetually suspended above the dark, frigid depths surrounding the docks. Seagulls floated in the air, riding the wind, squawking to one another in a never-ending chorus of delight, displeasure, or alarm. It was hard to tell which. I stood on the wharf, staring at the salmon and crab boats gently tugging at the salt-crusted ropes that bound them to the docks. A strong odor from previous catches rose from the rigging and from the nets spread about. In front of me, Dad marveled at the fleet of sturdy, battle-tested vessels. He was escaping again. This time his fantasy was to own one of those boats.

The solitude and purity of fishing have proved a lure that has caught countless thousands of fishermen and would-be fishermen, time and time again. Something primal and basic; the fisherman and his rig against the elements, against the fish. In snatches of conversation, I got the impression Dad thought those merciless, unforgiving seas, in testing his metal, would call him to life.

Maybe he was imagining how far it could take him from his problems: his failures, his family, the demons that pursued him. The truth was, he had no place left to run. No more options and no more alternatives. Only dreams held any hope of the success, the status he so desperately sought. Reality refused to comply.

We walked along the planks, stopping at nearly every boat, especially enjoying the names painted on the bow or stern, and wondering at the stories behind them. Names like *Straights, Sarah Mine, Star Northern,* and *Sea Mercy.* From row to row and dock to dock I followed my dad, wandering through the fog of his dreams.

The clang of ships bells and the long, low moan of the lighthouse whistle gave the boat slips and their vessels a lonely feeling. I acted interested but my enthusiasm paled in comparison to my father's. I felt sorry for him but somewhat relieved at the same time. Maybe the love of the idea of being a sea captain would be enough to replace the drinking. Whatever money the family had left, my father spent on fishing nets, licenses, gear and equipment.

Everything except a boat.

One day after several months there, on an ordinary early evening, on an ordinary street, at our ordinary home, my dad came home for the last time. He poured himself through the front door hardly able to stand or speak. My mother, my sister, and I stood in the hallway to watch the spectacle.

He was selling used cars during the day and at night he would stay drinking in seedy bars until they cut him off. For some reason, on that night my mom had finally had it. "You need to leave. Get out. We can't take anymore." Crying and sobbing, the man could only say how sorry he was; that he would try harder; "this was the last time." It was a familiar song, and we all knew the refrain. We'd heard it a million times.

This time, finally, it fell flat. We had all had enough. By then the raging, angry father I grew up knowing was reduced to a weak and frail full time drunk.

It was over.

So unthreatening was he that my mother started pushing him back out the door. He cried and pleaded for forgiveness clutching to the door frame. After that, he fell down and rolled slowly out of the house. The door was shut and locked behind him. Outside, the one-time tyrant wept and whimpered for a long time. Inside, three survivors huddled and wept, too.

It was a death in mourning for all. On either side of a hollow-core door, the crushing weight of disaster and failure finally played out. On one side, a soul completely lost to the inescapable loneliness of himself, and on the other, three souls, wounded and scared, listening in silence until the big bad wolf shuffled away.

Divorce followed. Dad was gone, the house was sold, and we moved to the poorer side of town. Over time we had gone from having everything to having barely enough to eat. To some extent the relief was worth it. Still, I was a fourteen year-old boy who no longer had a father. He had left me in more ways than I can even really comprehend. He left me physically, emotionally, and personally. But he was my dad; he was gone and my heart was broken.

It was a late 19th century home the three of us moved in to, in the old part of town near the railroad tracks. Dad had moved back to California, promising to send support. It never came, even when my mom called and begged. He always promised he would. Promises were currency he had plenty of, but they didn't buy shoes. When Mom told him mine had big holes in the soles, she was met with the same thing. Promises. She even reached out to her own parents, but they were unsympathetic. To them she was simply paying the price for marrying a man they had warned her about. Her suffering was exactly what they had told her to expect.

No new shoes.

Before long, I spent all my time alone again. My mother had found a boyfriend. She worked days and stayed at his house at night. The refrigerator collected mold and the house was layered thick with dust and cobwebs. I lost weight, getting thinner and thinner. I was going into 9th grade and nearing five feet eleven inches tall but I only weighed 130 pounds. My sister had abandoned ship as soon as possible. She'd joined the Army and was shipped off to Europe.

I'd watch TV, falling asleep on the couch. In the morning, I'd wake to find a note from my mother, together with a dollar bill.

It wasn't long before I started going to class less and less. At sixteen, I finally dropped out of school completely. Fortunately not before I found a miracle in a speech therapist. Finally, the lisp that plagued me all my life was corrected. Not before, however, it had done its sixteen years of damage to my self-esteem.

I soon fell into a crowd I could identify with, a subculture that lived as I did, problem kids, dropouts. I drifted, walking around downtown, often coming home just to the notes and dollar bills.

For a long time I was able to hide the fact I wasn't going to school. But eventually the inevitable happened and Mom found out. She resigned herself to the situation, realizing she had lost complete control of her son. We had grown apart, and I wasn't worth the bother. For a time she ceased to be an influence in my life. She had scars and so did I. We both had to deal with the past but we had to go about it independently.

One day while I was home there was a knock at the door. When I opened it, I was shocked to see my dad standing there. As soon as he set eyes on me, he started crying. Then came the same tired litany of apologies. Attached to each of them was some justification for the thing he was apologizing for. He needed me to see how bad off he was, as if that would absolve him for not ever helping.

Standing on the front steps I found myself comforting him. "It will be okay, Dad." Suddenly, I was the grown-up.

Maybe I always had been.

He went into the closet and rummaged through some old boxes, then he left. I seem to remember that he stayed in town for a few days, probably spending time with his drinking buddies. Looking back, I think the reason he came all that way was to show us how poor and pathetic he was, so my mom would stop bugging him for money. Anyway, next thing I knew, he was back in California, selling used cars, drinking himself into oblivion and living in a garage someone had converted into an apartment.

A new family moved in across the street. One of them was a kid about my age who always had his younger brother hanging around. One day he invited me to a youth group meeting. I didn't really know what that meant, just that it was a bunch of kids going to church. One thing I did know, they weren't like me.

And so, at six o'clock the following night I walked into a strange house full of unfamiliar kids. I felt like a dog at a funeral. It was a familiar feeling. I'd been the new kid many times.

Everyone knew each other. Lively talk and laughter were going on all around me. I was introduced and the more people I met, the more out of place and awkward I felt. Everyone seemed genuinely lighthearted and happy, full of fun. After a while, we all sat in a circle in the living room. Someone played the guitar and soon everyone was singing praise songs; songs I didn't know. I wasn't just a new kid; I was a foreigner in a strange land.

My wet jacket reeked of cigarettes. I felt unclean. At some point during the singing I slipped out of the circle and out the front door. I was so relieved to be out of that house. Our cultures were miles apart. I walked home, glad to light up a cigarette and find my other friends – those who spoke my language.

Maybe a seed was planted that night. I don't know. One thing stuck, though: the notion that Jesus was God's son, and he wanted to know me, to have a relationship with me.

I had a lot to go through before I was ready for that.

At the time, I was working part time in fast food restaurants. I felt discarded, a nobody, stranded to somehow make a life for myself. I didn't miss the fact that my parents didn't help me buy a car, or save money for college. I'd never considered the possibility. Not me.

Nor were they the kind of parents to prepare me for life in any practical way. I knew nothing about personal finance, money management, credit, paying bills, or taxes. The dark side of life, they showed me by example. They certainly didn't teach me about reaching my potential and living out my dreams either. I was on my own to figure things out.

Instinctively, probably taking a page from my father's book, I felt I had to be tough to survive. Though deep inside something had clicked, I was at least aware of Jesus – of gentleness: turning the other cheek. Maybe the friend from across the street prayed for me. Maybe the youth group did, too. But I stilled that voice. For me, Jesus would just have to hang on His cross a little while longer. I just needed a little more time.

One day I saw the movie *First Blood*. In it Sylvester Stallone portrayed Vietnam vet John Rambo, a character I could identify with. He was a drifter, haunting the highways and backroads of northwest Washington. The movie captured the damp and cold I was used to. Rambo captured me: a loner, sad and rootless. He lived guardedly and just wanted to be left alone.

Though capable of tenderness and civility, if anybody tried to hurt him, he knew how to defend himself. When he was in trouble, his survival skills and ability to adapt and improvise made him completely self-sufficient. At some deep level in my damaged psyche, he'd become my god.

I felt empowered when I imagined myself being known and respected. Like John Rambo, I knew I didn't want to be hurt anymore, I could ride that determination through the tough training it would take to win respect. My mind was made up. This would become my new identity. I had to become indestructible on my own.

At seventeen, I followed my sister into the Army.

Great! All my problems would go away!

Yea, right.

We most often see God's plans in retrospect. That's a good thing. If I'd had any inkling of the journey I was about to take, I'd have gone home, crawled into bed, pulled the covers over my head and stayed there.

Chapter Five

June 20, 1983 – I was on my way to Army Basic Training at Fort Dix, New Jersey. The 747 descended into the Philadelphia airport in the mid-afternoon. I'd never been on an airplane or even in an airport for that matter. It was busy and crowded. I couldn't find the baggage claim which, evidently, was beyond a maze of twisting concourses, shuttles, and terminal buildings.

I'd had no trouble getting into the Army, but I wasn't given the option for Green Beret training, which is what I wanted. The recruiter had told me I couldn't join that elite organization straight off the street. I would have to spend an initial part of my enlistment doing something else. Because I didn't score very well on the vocational skills test, or ASVAB as it was called, I was given the option of truck driver or parachute rigger. Of course, I was disappointed and a little upset too. But the offer included assignment to Europe where I was told I could retake the test.

Despite this inauspicious beginning, I still felt drawn to the Special Forces. Whatever happened, I was starting fresh. No longer a shoulder for my dad to cry on, or a whipping boy to take out his frustration and failure upon; I had taken control of my destiny.

After finding my bags and rereading my generic Army orders again, I realized they didn't make any more sense than when I first read them. And I couldn't figure out where I was supposed to go next, or what I was supposed to do when I got there. Eventually, I ended up at the ground transportation level flanked by departing shuttle buses. After asking everyone I could, I managed to find the shuttle that would take me to Fort Dix. Evidently, I had already missed a departure and had to wait for the last shuttle out.

The sun was starting to go down when my bus finally entered the front gates of Fort Dix. I could see formations of soldiers marching, running, and doing jumping jacks. They were repeating commands and counting out loud. There were parade fields, brick two story buildings, and Army trucks and jeeps driving by. It looked just like the Army should. No great surprise. I felt an unfamiliar sense of belonging and looked forward to the challenge. My initial experience with the Army would prove to be awkward and confusing though.

If I didn't know any better, I should have thought it stressful. I was already late, and I hadn't even gotten off the bus yet. To say I was naive would be putting it lightly. The bus dropped me off at the small station in the middle of the base. I stood there with my bags, as I watched the shuttle drive off billowing exhaust, and waited for whoever was supposed to be there to tell me what to do.

I soon learned the extreme economy of words used to inform or instruct soldiers. The person I was expecting never arrived. Instead, there was only silence. On the door of the small cinder block building that served as the bus stop was a sign: "Report Here."

Gathering facts, I learned, was like following little clues or breadcrumb trails. Curiosity led me through the swinging doors. A few benches with several dozen coats of Army "busy work" were on them. And on the wall were three phones hanging side by side. One was black, and its sign read "incoming." The next one was red, and it stated "outgoing." And the last one was green, and it said, "In processing." I stood staring at each one, then back to the last one, and again over to first one.

All I knew for sure was that I wasn't "outgoing." It was the other two that had me confused. Finally, I grabbed the green phone receiver, assuming green definitely meant Army. It was a 50/50 shot because the black phone also had an official look to it. I put the receiver to my ear, immediately a voice came on saying thirty seconds worth of name, rank, service number, duty station, duty position, and finally, "How may I assist you, Sir or Ma'am?" I hesitated and then replied, "My, my name is Don and I'm at the bus station and . . ."

Apparently that wasn't the right choice of words. The sergeant exploded, yelling some staccato commands from which I gathered someone would be coming to pick me up and, if his tone of voice was any indication, they would take me into the woods and shoot me.

The borders of the parking lot were designated by painted rocks. I stood there with my suitcases, and waited. Very soon, a military sedan pulled up and the occupants, two black soldiers, waved me over.

"Are you guys my ride?" I asked.

"Yeah. That's us. Jump in," one of them said.

In I jumped, and off we drove. Sitting in back, I noticed the MP arm bands the two of them wore. They made small talk as we slowly drove all over the base. I learned later that there was nothing worse than two bored military police sergeants on patrol. They could be surprisingly inventive.

Still unaware, I just waited patiently for them to take me wherever I was supposed to go. I answered a lot of questions with "Yeah" and "Uh huh" until one of them laughed and said "You'd better watch out. The Army don't like 'yeah' too much." The ride was a hazing of sorts, but if nothing else, that bit of advice served me well. As wrong as it was to drive me around in circles, they really did try to teach me a few things. They knew I just didn't know any better, but would be better off getting some subtle advice. 'Yeah' was scratched from my vocabulary, to be replaced by "Yes, Sir," or "Yes, Sergeant!"

Finally, we pulled up to a two story barracks building and they told me to go inside; there'd be someone there to take care of me. I thanked them and waved them off into the night. If I didn't know better, I'd have sworn they were giggling. (There's something weird and unnerving about two big, burly soldiers doing that.)

Inside the building I found a major sitting behind a desk, working late. He raised tired eyes to me and regarded me as if I was an apparition that had just materialized from another dimension. He didn't say anything, so I said: "I was dropped off to report here."

"You what? By who? Wait a minute. Why are you here?"

I struggled for an answer that would satisfy all the questions. "Basic Training?"

It was as if I'd set a match to the major's fuse. Angrily he reiterated the questions until I'd run through the sequence of events that had brought me there. It wasn't a long story and he seemed to pick up on the plot pretty quickly. He grabbed the rotary dial phone from his desk and with a lot of energy barked, "Reception station," at the operator. When that connection was made, the conversation went on about me as if they were talking about an inanimate object. Finally the major handed the inanimate object the phone, and the irate sergeant on the other end demanded to know why I hadn't waited for the van and, instead, drove off with two MP's?

"No one said a van was coming. They just said wait to be picked up, so that's what I did." The major rubbed his temples like he had a migraine. I was told to go outside and wait for the van. "Yes, Sir." I said into the phone. I thought that would make a good impression. "Yes, Sergeant," came the reply, emphasizing 'sergeant.' I corrected myself. "Yes, Sergeant." The sergeant hung up – without saying "Good-bye," or "Welcome to the Army. Great to have you."

The major slowly shook his head saying, "You know you're in trouble, right? You're five hours late." I shrugged and said, "I missed the bus."

That's when I learned that shrugging and making excuses were even worse than "Yeah" and "Uh-huh." When the major had related his thoughts on the topic, I said: "Yes, Sir. Sorry, Sir," and slunk outside. That phrase became central to my new vocabulary in the weeks and months to come.

The van pulled up, and I got in and received an ear full all the way back to the Basic Training Reception Station. There the Sergeant I had spoken to on the phone picked up where the driver left off and let me know his pretty rigid opinions about being on time, and not getting "lost all over the place." He also shared his thoughts about the MPs who had given me the run-around. I decided to keep my thoughts to myself.

This guy, I learned in short order, was the reception sergeant and there was more than a little of my dad in his attitude. Whether or not he'd hit me remained to be seen. Finally, though, he settled down and sent me off to the cafeteria, where I ate a meal more or less in the dark. I don't recall that introduction to Army cuisine – it might as well have been sawdust for all I noticed.

Afterward, I was escorted through a maze of corridors and hallways to a set of double doors where several intimidating looking soldiers were waiting. They were standing in a semi-circle around a weight scale. I felt like a new convict, newly arrived at the cell block. I didn't have a lot of experience with other ethnicities, but that was about to change.

These guys, it became apparent, were accustomed to processing large numbers of inductees at a time. Here I was, late, alone, chalky white and green as a ripe avocado. They, on the other hand, were decidedly not chalky white, and they all seemed at least two feet bigger than me, both in height and shoulder-width, and I was about to get their undivided attention.

One of them walked over to me and – though I was actually taller, he still seemed to look down at me. "Strip private," he said, his face as cold as stone. I gulped and, with slow moving hands, reached for my belt buckle. Another few seconds of poker-faced silence followed, then they all suddenly burst out laughing. "Just kidding, man," said the Sergeant, grabbing me by the shoulder he pulled me to the scale. "Step on up here, Skinny."

I did what I was told and manufactured a feeble smile to hide my discomfort. I wasn't in training yet, but I'd already learned an important operating principle of the Army: put sudden fear into people. Once that had been accomplished your tormentors often became your saviors, usually to the accompaniment of good-natured laughter. The exercise nurtured a kind of camaraderie. It was a love-hate kind of thing.

To top the night off for great first impressions, it was one a.m. when I was brought to my barracks. The sergeant flipped on the light and seven other bunkees were suddenly awakened. The door slammed behind us and I slunk to the only vacant bunk. What I wanted, more than anything at that moment, was to be invisible. The sergeant had other plans. "This is private Kabrich," he announced. "He's late. Make him comfortable."

With that he flicked off the light and left, letting the door slam behind him like a big exclamation point. Without unpacking or undressing, I lay down on my bunk, trying to keep the springs from squeaking. I closed my eyes and, to a chorus of unhappy mumbles, fell instantly into a deep sleep. I had survived my first three hours in the United States Army – just barely. My 'invisible man' approach hadn't gone according to plan.

Bang! bang! bang! Garbage can lids hit the walls.

I was stunned awake. It felt like I'd just closed my eyes, but a glance at my watch informed me that three and a half hour had passed. The florescent lights overhead were turned on, and drill sergeants were yelling at us trainees to get outside "Now!"

I sprang off my bunk and hit the floor. Everyone was racing by me and out the door. I couldn't open my eyes more than half-way; the lights were too bright. I kept trying to force them open. Bleary-eyed, I veered toward the door. I'd been in the Army just over seven hours and was on my way to being late for the second time.

In what I could see through the sleep-fog of my vision, the barracks looked like a bomb had gone off in it. Lockers stood open, blankets and pillows hung half on and half off the beds, papers littered the floor – some of them bearing official Army insignia. What more could they expect? We'd been given thirty seconds to get out of the room. That's how novices typically respond to the shock of their first roll call. We were official, certifiable screw ups. Just the kind of raw material the Army likes from which to mold soldiers.

Mission accomplished.

The eight weeks of basic training passed in a blur. For the most part, the daily routine consisted of marching – lots of marching – learning to fire a rifle, kitchen duty (KP), and cleaning stuff: from barracks and rifles, to kitchens and latrines. Everything had to be done in double-time and failure to pay attention to details brought punishment on the entire platoon.

It was late June when classes began, and it felt like a hundred percent humidity outside. For a west coast boy – used to a climate so dry it was almost brittle – this came as a shock, like I was in a tropical rain forest. I half expected to hear monkeys in the trees.

I needed to acclimate quickly, so I did.

I seized this opportunity to make a fresh start. In the course of that eight weeks, I discovered hidden strengths. I learned to project confidence – toughness and strength – even if, inside, I didn't feel it, I'd proved to myself that I had the capacity to grow into that image. That was a valuable, if not obvious, lesson; the desire to be great at something doesn't

make you great at it. That's just the vision. What makes it real is hours, weeks, days, and years of hard work. And that takes raw determination, the expectation that it was going to be hard, and the determination to hang in there when it was.

It probably sounds poetic to say I'd turned a page in my life, but that's what it felt like. Not just a new page, a new chapter. My old life with all its pain and chaos faded into a background of memories that grew more distant every day. I thought they were dying. I later learned they'd just been buried alive.

For now, though, I'd established a new life; one of

order, clarity, and purpose.

I took to the Army well, learned quickly, and was highly motivated. The reward structure, with its clearly defined ladder of duties and goals was perfect for me. As I created a brand new life, I gained the respect of both my peers and those above my pay grade, and that respect grew into a good reputation as a savvy, dependable soldier: a leader.

I always went the extra mile in everything I did. I ran harder, yelled louder, and impressed the drill sergeants with my natural military bearing. I sought leadership and took charge whenever I could. I aspired to be the trainees' student platoon leader, but those with prior service and college credit got that privilege. Where others shied away from responsibility, I craved it. The drill sergeants sensed that and gave me the coveted position of guidon bearer. The platoon's distinctive flag led the way wherever we went. I raised, spun, thrust, and paraded it constantly. No one could do it better and I knew it. That guidon was the banner leading the way, and I carried it.

That position went a long way toward satisfying my earliest ambitions in the Army. I was extremely proud. As far as I was concerned I had become the platoon's symbol of excellence, and I'd earned it.

If it wasn't for the small facing movement mistake made by the drill sergeant, our platoon would have won the coveted "best marching platoon" competition. Our platoon had practiced to the point of being as tight as a school of fish, or a flock of birds. The grandstands audibly "wowed" when they saw our formation. Like one fluid action, single slides and clicks of weapons bolts were being released, as we performed a several count check; "Inspection Arms." We would have made any Presidential honor guard proud.

However, It was the command of "right face" that did us in. It turns out, you can't give a facing movement when the weapons are at "shoulder arms." Marching back, our drill sergeant kicked himself in the butt all the way back to the company area; he'd let us down.

Chapter Six

After several weeks of basic training my motivation and enthusiasm became obsession. Staying up late, I'd deprive myself of much-needed sleep. After all the lights were out I'd shine my boots and tighten up my bunk. I slept on top of the covers so mine would be the first feet to hit the floor in the morning. Then, while the others were crawling out from under their covers, I'd make a couple of quick passes over the blanket with the flat of my hand, and my bunk was inspection-ready. I'd learned that trick the first few days of in-processing.

In time the grueling pace I set myself caught up with me. A sinus cold turned into an infection, which turned into bronchitis, which eventually turned into pneumonia. Still, for as long as I could, I hid my condition.

One day I could tell my temperature had risen dangerously high. I needed an aspirin to lower it. Every morning at the end of formation the drill sergeant would announce "sick call." And each time dozens of guys got sheepishly in line only to be sent back humiliated and embarrassed. I hated it, but I had to get in that line to get medical help or my temperature was going to fly through the roof.

As the line shuffled forward each trainee would present his issue and be immediately yelled at and sent back into the ranks. I got to the front of the line. The sergeant looked at me and after a moment said, "You better go see the medic." Obviously I looked as bad as I felt. I was the only trainee sent for further evaluation.

I walked a short distance to the medical vehicle, designated by a big red cross on a white background. There, a medic put a thermometer in my mouth. When he took it out and read it he looked at me with a sudden expression of grave concern. He whispered a few words to his buddy and any chance of my getting a simple aspirin was quickly smashed. An ambulance was backed up, I was flung inside, a surgical mask slapped on me, and then raced off to the Army hospital. My temperature was 105 degrees and my lungs were full of rust-like colored infection.

I'd been walking around with pneumonia for a week or two.

It was week seven of training and I was no longer with my platoon. In a hospital gown lying in a hospital bed I continued to run a fever and cough up rust colored phlegm. I was on powerful antibiotics but they were not working fast enough. My drill sergeant stopped by to see how I was doing and to tell me I would most likely have to repeat the last few weeks of training. Testing was in two days and that was a "must pass" phase of basic training.

After he left, I tried to will my body to recover quicker. It didn't work. Every two hours my temperature was taken and the nurses would collect a sample of what I coughed up. Every time yielded the same result. I had a temperature of 103 and continued to cough. I heard from another patient that if my temperature was lower and I was not coughing anything up I could be released. It didn't take long for me to formulate a plan. Not graduating on time was not an option. I had to get back to training and my final testing.

For two days I sucked on ice chips and coughed up whatever I could before the nurses arrived. And, not so miraculously, my temperature decreased and my lungs seemed to have cleared up. By day two I was cleared and was given permission to get back to training. With no time to spare, I threw on my uniform and ran out the front doors of the hospital. Time was so short between my release and the start of testing that I didn't even feel there was time to organize a ride back.

Still having a temperature and pneumonia in my lungs I ran, walked, jogged and stumbled five miles back to my training area. By the time I got there testing had already begun. Understanding my situation, all the testing stations accepted my lateness. To be honest there were a few stations I did not know how to pass at all. I had missed a few important briefings. Sweating and sick, breathing with a rasp in my chest, I managed to get through all the final testing stations in the nick of time.

Five days later, on the 20th of August, I stood on the parade grounds at the front of the platoon. I graduated basic training still holding the heart and soul of the platoon – the guidon which I hoped reflected its character on me.

After graduation, we marched back to the company area singing cadence all the way. The long eight weeks of training were finally over. What I didn't know was that I'd just earned myself *another* eight weeks.

As our basic training drill sergeant finished his last formation with us, another one took his place. He was our Advanced Individual Training (AIT) drill instructor. Most of my platoon-mates were going to transportation school, and our break between Basic Training and AIT was mostly over.

The drill instructor with his Smoky the Bear hat called "Right face! Forward march!" Myself and the twenty or so other soldiers picked up our two heavy duffel bags and started down the endless rows of training barracks. We were not told how far we were going, so we carried our duffel bags just the way we had hastily picked them up. Instead of carrying them a short distance, we endured screaming muscle pain and strain for a couple of miles.

We had arrived at our new training area, and the barracks were carbon copies of one another; it was like the movie *Groundhog Day* except with an even more nightmarish quality. As a total morale killer, the new drill sergeants treated us as bad or worse than our previous instructors. An hour after our introduction to our new D.I., I was already in trouble. Push-ups and jumping jacks were dished out as punishment. The shouts of abuse, the routine of manufacturing enthusiasm, were to be repeated. Eight more weeks of man-made suffering.

Welcome to the Army.

After a long day of being transferred from down the road, we were finally released for a day and half of free time. The free time could only be spent in the barracks, chow hall, and surrounding company area.

Welcome to AIT.

Thus far, throughout my ordeals in life, I'd never really thought to ask God for help. Even though I had a drive-by acquaintance with religion and some born-again Christians, I still had no understanding of who God was. Since, back in the youth group days, I had rejected becoming a Christian and opted to go it alone, because that's what heroes do. To me, it seemed those Christians I encountered from time-to-time wanted me to give up all of my heroic hopes, dreams, and vices in order to accept God in my life.

If ever I accepted God, it would have to be on *my* terms, not His. When He was ready to fall in line, great, until then I had plans, and I fully intended to work them out.

I supposed that, through all the negative experiences in my life, I did pray after a fashion, but those prayers would have been more 'if-then' blackmail demands that I'd launch into the universe, each with an unspoken addendum: "Be kind to me." I didn't much care what cosmic force caught those prayers, as long as they came through. Like SETI, I was scattering my message – my appeals – to anyone out there who might be listening.

They were prayers in search of a god.

Until they were answered to my satisfaction, my theology would be: it's easier to ask for forgiveness than permission. In other words, I'd do whatever I felt I needed to do in order to bring my plans online and, if at the end I needed forgiveness for something, I'd ask for it.

Meantime, I wanted what I wanted and I wasn't going to let God get in the way. Surrender, of the kind He required, was simply not in the cards.

We were back at square one. Monday morning we were given another physical fitness test. It sounded crazy, since we had literally just come from Basic Training. However, because of my walking pneumonia, my physical fitness level had actually been seriously affected. Just eight weeks before, I could run two miles in eleven minutes. I concluded AIT physical training test with a run time of nineteen minutes. Truth is, I was still pretty sick, and I'd probably left the hospital two weeks too soon.

So, the remedy for this discrepancy in my time trials was additional physical fitness training; the exact opposite of what I needed, which was more rest, not additional miles to run. But there was nothing I could do about it. I was in the Army, and without rank. I'd just have to suck it up. Or die.

At the time, my dad was dating a woman named Irene. She learned about my situation and sent me some antibiotics and they helped jump start my recovery. Not before however, I had one of my worst days of training in the hot and humid August sun. Left standing in formation for what seemed like hours, one of my co-trainees, a big guy with a loud mouth, started complaining in the ranks. Everyone was afraid the drill sergeant would hear – and we'd all have to pay. Still, because the guy had a violent reputation – recently he'd stomped a guy's face for some real or imagined offense – no one told him to shut up.

But I was sick as a dog and didn't particularly care, at that moment, what might happen to me. I laid into the big guy. If anyone had a reason to whine, it was me. Basically, I told him to shut up and stop complaining; that he would get everyone in trouble. If looks could kill I'd have died on the spot. He was looking around to see if he could deck me without the DI seeing. In the end he just snarled "I'll kill you."

In the back of my mind, to make matters worse, was the awareness that he'd just been transferred to my room. It felt like prison politics, and someone was gonna get "stuck." Probably me.

Later that day, steeling myself to face the music, I walked into my barracks and to my wall locker. When I turned around, I found myself face-to-face with my would-be assassin. He grabbed me by the collar and lifted me a foot off the ground. I wasn't prepared, either mentally or physically, to fight. I just wanted to get the beating over with.

I'd been beat before.

I was slammed against the locker. I mumbled an apology – doing my best to bury the hatchet before it got buried in my head. Surprisingly, the guy started to settle down and seemed to accept what I was saying. A few moments later, he let me down and warned me to keep my comments to myself or the next time he wouldn't let me off the hook.

To be honest, the guy was probably so shocked that I would just walk in and take whatever came against obviously uneven odds, that he wound up respecting my courage. Besides, we had to be roommates. In the end, the mysterious alchemy of military bonding worked its magic and we became pretty good friends.

Speaking of magic, the antibiotics killed the last of the infection and I felt much better. Throughout the remaining eight weeks, I learned how to drive everything from jeeps to eighteen-wheelers. As far as Advanced Training went, it was pretty interesting. After all, I was being paid to drive jeeps, four wheeling through mud and up steep hills. I also finally got a chance to lead. I had made my way up to the position of platoon leader.

My ability to march the formation and lead the cadence songs made getting the job a lot easier. Just a few short months earlier, I thought myself a nobody with no future. Now I was marching whole formations of soldiers on one of the United States Army's largest training bases. I had done it. I had reinvented myself.

Before long, I was no longer just a wounded, boy-shaped victim of my father's abuse. I had become a man – capable of standing on my own two feet – challenging myself and rising to that challenge. I had earned a place of respect amongst my peers and, in time, received a letter of appreciation for my performance as platoon guide. That letter hangs on the wall in my study to this day.

That was still in the future. For the time being I had to get through AIT – which basically meant struggling for eight weeks to survive the DI's attempts to kill me. That's how it felt. However, after sixty-four more days of climbing, crawling, running, marching, shooting, being left for long periods of time to bake in the scorching sun and learning how to function as part of a team, I graduated. At the conclusion of a brief ceremony marking the event, I learned that my first duty station would be Germany.

Chapter Seven

Heidelberg, Germany

The bus rolled slowly through the low hanging fog and onto the small US military *kaserne* (German for barracks) where I was to be stationed. At the edge of town sat Patton Barracks – originally a German military post that had been taken over by General Patton's army in the aftermath of World War II. For the most part, it looked pretty much like it had back in the 1940's.

Large, well-established pine trees dotted the courtyards and several of them surrounded the parade field. Its center was a cement circle, in the middle of which stood a tall pole with a large American flag, whipping in the wind. This, too, was a strange contrast. Peering out the bus window through the mist, I tried to draw the scene into focus. I felt a strange sense of loneliness, of the unfamiliar, and didn't have to work to imagine the ghosts of WWII wandering that same property, bent beneath their own duffle bags and the heavy judgment of history.

Oddly, I felt ready. I was trained and disciplined, boots shined and uniform pressed. I was used to living in strict and rigid military environments, so whatever happened I felt equipped to handle it.

Most of the buildings were three-story barracks that the U.S. Army had adapted for peacetime purposes. These modifications aside, if not for the American flags on the sides of the vehicles and uniforms, it would be easy to imagine the place still a hive of German wartime activity. Narrow cobblestone streets separated the neat rows of buildings, some of which still barracked a small company of German soldiers.

The bus stopped. I stepped off and immediately was aware of a less tense environment. To start with, no one began yelling at us when we got off the bus, and the corporal of the 501st Transportation Company who met us and led the way to the barracks seemed almost relaxed. As he conducted us on a quick familiarization tour of the facility, he was almost friendly. He kept up a running commentary that seemed more impromptu than practiced and perfunctory. As a footnote he informed us that, it being the weekend, the place was pretty quiet.

Inside the barracks, I was in for a shock. The long hallways, punctuated with doors every few feet, were dirty, dingy, and dark. A startling contrast from what I was used to. Even more alarming, soldiers sat around half-dressed, their uniforms disheveled and mixed with civilian clothes. Cigarette smoke filled the air and large floor fans distributed it evenly around the room, so that those who didn't smoke were sure to get just as much in their lungs as those who did.

The corporal motioned for us to follow him upstairs. On the second floor just around the corner, he stopped and knocked on the first door. Thumping music vibrated from within. The door opened and an overweight, smiling soldier, clearly drunk, said "Whassup?" The corporal turned to us. "Men, let me introduce you to the company First Sergeant." To a brand new troop it was like meeting the highest ranking drill sergeant. Caught off guard, I immediately reacted by straightening up. Just as quickly, the sloppy drunk said, laughing "What? Nah, nah. I ain't the First Sergeant. He's just trying to trip y'all out."

At our expense – and in keeping with Army tradition – they enjoyed a hearty laugh. "Just kidding. First Sergeant's never around here." I couldn't believe what I was seeing. All my hard training and discipline, for what? The place reminded me of the movie *Animal House*.

Within a few months I'd settled in, made friends, got used to things, and had an established routine driving supply trucks around Heidelberg. Each afternoon after work, everyone would meet at the enlisted club to grab a bite and drink German beer. Being nineteen in Germany and of legal age, I did not have enough discipline to avoid staying up late. Often, my friends and I would get three or four hours sleep before having to get up for the daily 0530 morning formation.

Even though I had nothing but bad experiences surrounding alcohol, somehow drinking German beer didn't seem so bad. Besides, I was struggling with having been assigned to an army unit that didn't seem to demand much in the way of discipline and, as a result, attracted less enthusiastic soldiers. I tried to make the best of things, tried to fit in and, admittedly, enjoyed being in a relaxed military environment. But something inside demanded more; there were things I still had to prove – to myself, and to the world. John Rambo haunted the wilderness reaches of my mind. I still harbored that resolution to become the ultimate soldier. And the one thing I kept constantly thinking about was my own father's experience in the Army. All the rambling, drunken stories had made an impact on me.

My dad had compensated for his diminutive stature by standing out in his own way – winning inspections for the two years he served, 1959 to 1961. I was determined to do the same – and then some. I was determined to do better than he ever did. I needed to prove him wrong. To prove that I wasn't stupid, or weak, or worthless. In my heart I still basked in the glow of being chosen platoon guide in AIT. I wanted to keep the momentum going.

A strange dichotomy developed in me. At night I was just one of the guys: ordinary and unremarkable, but during work hours I was all spit-and-polish, contrasting sharply to my compatriots. Every night I shined my boots until I could

shave in their reflection. I'd spray starch, crease, and iron my fatigues. I carried myself the way I looked and felt. Taking it further, I'd wax and polish the floor, keeping it perpetually ready for inspection.

On occasion, the company would hold an inspection in formation or hold a contest for "soldier of the month." Knowing military history, current events, regulations, and military operating procedures were all tested. One at a time, we'd enter the room where a panel of our immediate superiors was convened. They began by asking several questions. Then we'd be judged on appearance and military bearing. Whenever these inspections or boards were conducted, I'd try to win – which meant earning a four-day pass or extra privileges.

The unintended rewards were far greater though. Heidelberg was the headquarters of USAREUR, United States Army European Command. The highest ranking enlisted position at the post was Command Sergeant Major, and he needed a new driver. When I was recommended, I attributed my selection, at least in part, to the fact that I looked the part, which would reflect well on him.

Just like that, overnight, I went from washing the mud off trucks and topping off oil in the motor pool, to sitting in a large professional office with fine china, classic European decor, surrounded by high-ranking personnel. I was only a lowly PFC (Private First Class), but I was suddenly responsible for transporting the USAREUR Command Sergeant Major!

A spit shine never went so far, so fast.

From the barracks, I'd walk a path about two miles to the headquarters building. The Command Sergeant Major's office was on one side of the top floor. Across from that was the office of the four-star general in charge of all of Europe. The highest-ranking military official on the continent.

Conference rooms, dining rooms, sculptures, wood carved doors, and artistic wall pieces occupied the second floor. On the first floor were more offices, the basement, though, seemed more like I imagined the Pentagon to be; there were secret communications rooms, endless corridors from which more offices, meeting, briefing and communications rooms, as well as a library and map room branched north and south. There was also a barber shop, a convenience store, and the cafeteria.

Headquarters was a city unto itself.

One day, after several weeks of driving the Sergeant Major to local events and meetings, his secretary told me the Sergeant Major needed to go to Nijmegen, Holland. He said I had to make a plan and be ready to depart in a few days.

I wound my way down the wide staircase and into the warren of secret hallways in the basement where I discovered the vast library of resources in the map room.

My adrenaline was already pumping in anticipation of suddenly being given so much responsibility.

I opened the large sliding map drawers and drew out a map of Europe. I put my index finger on Heidelberg and, with the other hand, the other index finger on Nijmegen, Holland. It was the entire length of a standard European map away! Looking at the distance between my fingers, another rush of adrenaline coursed through my body. I needed to deliver the second highest-ranked enlisted soldier safely to a destination several hundred kilometers away. I couldn't make a mistake.

I pulled out map after map. The scale got smaller and more detailed. Soon I was piecing together a detailed route noting roads, intersections, fuel points, safe travel, security, landmarks, and exact distances between way points. From point A to point B, I would have to seamlessly negotiate the European landscape. I couldn't get lost, couldn't stop and ask for directions, needed to establish specific refueling stations, and generally give the impression that cruising around Europe at between eighty and one hundred miles per hour was second nature.

Remember, these were pre-GPS days. There were no cell phones, much less Google maps. The only way to get around was with a good old paper map.

Along the way, every sign would be in another language, so there was no room for error or moments of relaxation. Not only would I have to get my passenger to the city of Nijmegen, but also to a pinpoint location within. From coordinating personnel to receive the Sergeant Major all the way to reserving lodging, I was in charge of it all. I made strip maps, took notes and made numerous phone calls. Seemingly overnight, I went from a simple truck driver to what felt like my own mini secret service detail.

On the day of the trip I was ready. My boots were polished to a high shine and my uniform was pressed with liberal amounts of starch. The assigned vehicle, a dark gray Granada Ghia, was in its parking space, equally shined, polished, and ready to go. It had a 2.8 liter, fuel-injected engine, power windows and sunroof, a Blaupunkt stereo and car phone. It was sleek; an American version of a four door Mercedes sedan. On my sun visor was a list of the Sergeant Major's frequently called and important numbers. While driving at high speeds, I was expected to serve as switchboard operator as well, ready to send and receive calls at a moment's notice.

If anyone liked intense jobs blended with a touch of cool, it was me. This was the dream job I'd never dreamed of! Heady as I felt, though, I was too young and naive to really appreciate the opportunity that had just dropped in my lap. At nineteen, I was just going with the flow, and the flow said this job gave me the opportunity to prove myself.

With one notable exception, I carried out the assignment flawlessly – safely and efficiently transporting the Sergeant Major to and from the Nijmegen Combined Forces March. More about that later. I dialed numbers without crashing, followed the route I had carefully laid out on my maps, stayed on the road, didn't get pulled over by traffic cops, and arrived on time at each stop along the way.

Wherever we pulled up, a contingent of support staff and VIPs would be there to meet the Sergeant Major. I'd hop out, step smartly around the car to open his door, and off he'd go surrounded by a little cloud of low and mid-level functionaries, several of whom glanced back at me over their shoulders. I imagined they couldn't believe a kid was in my position which was, relative to driving a supply truck, one of power and influence.

On the drive the Sergeant Major and I spent many hours in close company. If anyone had the Old Man's ear, it was me. That first night, in my hotel room, I was feeling pretty cocky and self-important. I slept well.

Too well.

The next morning, there was a knock at my door. My eyes flew open and drew the bedside alarm clock into focus. I was late! I jumped out of bed, threw on my uniform, ran downstairs and out to the car, beside which the Sergeant Major paced, highly agitated.

I muttered an apology as I unlocked and opened his door, but I didn't make any excuses. "My fault, Sergeant Major. It won't happen again."

And it wouldn't, even if it meant I never slept again.

Fortunately, that was the only mistake I made on the trip. Disaster had been avoided and, when we returned to base, I was informed that the Sergeant Major wanted to keep me on as his driver.

In the year I drove for him, there was only one other time I felt my luck had run out. I was transporting the Sergeant Major and his wife to an official function and we were delayed for hours, in traffic. In those days, the Autobahn – Germany's much-vaunted national highway system – was famous for the fact that it didn't have a speed limit.

That day it didn't need one.

The only thing moving was the fuel gauge. It got so low that the alarm kept sounding. I quickly mashed the button to silence it, but my eyes were glued to that gauge, willing the needle not to sink any lower. At one point, I looked in the rear-view mirror and caught the Sergeant Major's eyes. He knew what was happening.

I could read those eyes. They said: "If we run out of gas with Mrs. Sergeant Major, we will have a problem." By which he meant *I* would have a problem. Vivid pictures of exactly what shape that problem might take rushed into my mind. I could feel the sweat forming on my brow as, whenever I could, I'd put my foot on the clutch and coast.

Finally, the traffic jam eased up and we drove onto the

base. As calmly as I could, still holding my breath, I delivered the couple to their destination. I limped to the fuel stop on fumes. I could almost hear the engine gasping. For every litre that went in, as I filled the tank, I felt an equal amount of weight lift from my shoulders.

One of the last places I took the Sergeant Major left a chilling and indelible image in my mind that haunts me still.

I knew something was up. I wasn't told in advance where we were going, just to be fully fueled, as we drove, the Sergeant Major gave me directions and ultimately we ended up at a missile base. It was 1985 and the Cold War was still going strong.

The base itself was fairly innocuous from the outside. Inside, it was a different story. Here, the Cold War was in your face. We passed through several high-level security points, each manned by heavily armed and deadly serious MPs, at each of which credentials were carefully checked, even though most of the guards seemed to know the Sergeant Major on sight.

Rounding a final corner upon arriving at our destination, the reason for the security became evident: pointing at the sky – and arching toward Moscow – stood a picket-fence of pointy-tipped missiles a hundred feet high. Their deadly, unspoken purpose seemed to weigh on the atmosphere. People talked in low voices and whispers, as if too much noise would set them off. This wasn't a movie. Standing in their ominous presence was surreal. The missiles felt almost alive, like untamed beasts ready to pounce at the slightest provocation.

Most chilling of all was the knowledge that, not far away in the vastness of the Soviet system, similar arrays equally prepared to pounce, were aimed in our direction.

That was my introduction to reality on a global scale, and a sharp slap in the face.

Up until then, I'd just been going with the flow, and the

universe seemed indifferent to my plans. Just three short years earlier I had had a lisp, no food, no money and, as a high school dropout, no prospects.

Now look at me! Spit and polish, trusted, respected, no lisp, money in my pocket, and the respect of my superiors.

But my father's demon had tracked me down and camped at my door. I'd developed a drinking problem and didn't even know it. Or at least wouldn't admit it. My dad was the one with the drinking problem – the posterchild for AA, not me.

One night I had CQ or Charge of Quarters duty, meaning I had to stay up all night manning the office and answering the phone. I was sitting alone when an older soldier in civilian clothes stopped into chat – which was not a common occurrence. From his bearing I figured he was probably an officer or higher ranking enlisted guy, and very friendly.

He struck up a conversation and before I knew it, was asking if I went to church! It was happening again. Out of nowhere, these people were poking their sticks in the spokes of my life. Why me? How did they find me? Why did they care about me, or my soul?

But they kept showing up, and I kept turning them away. I had no interest in what they were selling.

This time was different. First of all, I couldn't be sure of this guy's rank, so I had to tread carefully in my responses to his questions. He asked if I had a relationship with Jesus; if I knew whether I was going to heaven or not? He wanted me to go to church with him and his family. I politely refused the offer. After an hour or so, he left, and I never saw him again.

Today I wonder if that soldier – and the others who had approached me in Jesus' name – were really angels in disguise.

Did angels have families?

Looking back, knowing what I know now, it really impresses me how that guy took what little free time he had to come to talk to me – a complete stranger – in a lonely posting in the middle of the night.

That took every bit as much courage as facing the enemy on the physical battlefield. In battle, nothing's personal. It's just you or your opponent and that's it. On the spiritual battlefield, though, with no idea how I'd respond, he had laid down all his defenses, opening himself to rebuke, or ridicule, in any event rejection at a personal and intimate level.

Once more, in retrospect, just as I had when I'd walked out of that youth group meeting years before, I wonder how different my subsequent life would have been had I taken him up on his invitation.

However, just as I had before, I left Jesus hanging up there on His cross.

Chapter Eight

After eighteen months it was time to return to Fort Hunter Liggett, California to finish my three-year enlistment. When I got out, since I was back in my home state and Uncle Sam would foot the bill, I decided to go to college. By then my parents had, independently, moved back to San Jose. I had a lot of family there so making the transition to civilian life figured to be pretty straightforward. In reality, it turned out that I was all alone in a city full of family and friends.

I didn't reach out. I left the reaching out to them, not really expecting that they would, which would justify my feelings of rejection.

What can I say? I was still a kid. Still afraid of being beaten or abandoned one way or another. So I beat them to the punch.

Getting out of the Army isn't just a simple case of walking away. Leadership won't sign-off on your out-processing paperwork without interviewing you and asking your plans once you get out. Since most GIs don't have a job waiting for them, college is an acceptable alternative and speaks volumes about the likelihood that you'll make the most of your opportunity to better yourself.

Educationally, I had a lot of catching up to do, so I enrolled in West Valley College in Saratoga, California, determined to regain ground I had lost by being a high school dropout.

I continued to have drinking problems. One was never enough. I got in trouble for drunk driving and everything was falling apart. On top of that, I owned nothing but the broken down car I lived in at times. I had no home, no job, and no family, really. I slept in the parking lot at Denny's, scrounged for nickels and dimes under my car seat, and lost weight because I didn't eat regularly. My 'friends' were the kind that could always be counted on, as long as I had money. Otherwise, they were nowhere to be found.

From 1986 to 1995, when I left California, I'd lived in fourteen or more places and had an equal number of jobs.

Life had become one long pity party.

Still, I told myself I was tough. I'd survived the Army – even excelled there. It had made me callous. I wanted nothing more than to be respected – not the kind of respect that comes to someone naturally because they've earned it, but the kind that comes from instilling fear. Like John Rambo, I could be deadly, a force to be reckoned with. No one would hurt me again.

I'd cauterize those old wounds until, under the scabs, they'd heal.

That was my prescription.

Apparently those wounds weren't as well hidden as I imagined. It seemed like everywhere I turned a Christian would pop up out of nowhere and start talking to me about God.

I resisted because I thought Jesus was meek and mild, and so were His followers. Those weren't attributes that fit into my survival plan, which was to be physically and emotionally tough as nails.

Surrendering to Christ would be just another failure, acknowledgment that I was unable to stand on my own two feet; proving Dad right.

The truth is that, emotionally, I was about as tough as a damp rag and, it turned out, as transparent as glass. Drink brought my emotions to the surface and, in that fragile mental state, the years of childhood abuse were catching up to me. Depression had me in its grip. It began with waves of depression and fear that would descend on my soul without warning. I had difficulty staying in one place, keeping a job, or holding on to anything solid.

Echoes of John Rambo.

I could survive almost anything, except my childhood.

Fortunately, I found a temporary job – called a 'short tour,' typically ninety days – working at an Army Reserve unit and it was not long before God started banging on my head again. This time, He sent Harold Vanhaulder, a.k.a. "Mr. Van," to witness to me. He gave me things to read and some cassette tapes to listen to, and some of them got me thinking. They said things like, "Do you need to get cleaned up to take a bath?" In other words, what if God could take me just as I was. I did not have to give up anything or change first. The guy on the tape said change would come later, all I had to do was ask Him to come into my life, exactly where I was, as I was.

My short tour consisted of handling the thousands of items needing to be serviced and inventoried in a limited number of days before a deadline. And since reservists only served on weekends, and the full-time staff was extremely limited, they sometimes were allowed to enlist reservists to help complete specific, time sensitive missions.

It turned out that our higher command headquarters needed help with data processing. Thousands of items needed to be updated in the personnel computer. This data included things like place of residence, marriage date, promotion date, middle name, etc. When I heard about the opportunity of a ninety-day service opportunity coming available while I was attending one of my drill weekends, I signed up and was selected for the assignment.

The 353rd Civil Affairs Command wasn't too far from where I was living. There I was employed in the personnel section, which is where I met Chief Warrant Office (CW4) Van, administrative specialist for the Army and a full-time Army Reserves soldier; he was also a very strong Christian. His job was personnel management. He supervised much of the work I did.

While there the full-time position for Information

Management Officer (IMO) became available. It was called an AGR position. It stands for Active Guard Reserve. It is a civilian government position that requires you to serve on weekend drills. I applied for the position and waited. It was a GS-08 position (that is the grade or civilian rank). Most people have to start out in government at a GS-04 position but since I had already been working there I would be able to start at this more mid-level manager position. As IMO, I would be responsible for the command and seventeen subordinate units managing information: FAX and postal machines, copiers, computers, telephones bills, paper count, classified document storage and handling etc.

Before getting this position though – through Mr. Van – God kept reaching out to me.

Once again, I rebelled.

But in 1989, on New Year's Eve, penniless, all but jobless – my short tour being over and income gone – I waited to learn if I had gotten the full-time position. Mostly homeless, with my only possessions recently stolen from my car, I tracked down my dad and he let me stay in his one room apartment. I couldn't use the couch because he was usually passed out on it, so I slept on the floor. It was either that or my car.

New Year's Eve - 1989

The clock struck midnight and I could hear the celebration and joy throughout the neighborhood. I stood in the middle of the darkened room, and looked from my father, senseless on the dirty sofa, to my own pathetic, under-nourished, sad-eyed reflection in the window, through which – in the distance – fireworks lit up the sky.

Some Rambo.

I'd reached the end. The grand destiny I'd imagined for myself during those glory days in the Army had come to ashes.

I walked out onto the small balcony and stared up, searching the night for a glimpse of God. As I did, tears pooled in my eyes, and I heard myself say, "Please help me, God. I need you." I couldn't avoid Him any longer.

It was the first time I'd ever really stopped and spoke out so deliberately and personally to God, acknowledging Him as my Creator. Those few words unleashed a flood that unexpectedly welled up from hidden depths. Suddenly I was weeping aloud. "I don't know what to believe or where You are, but I need Your help. Please help me! I am sorry for the things I've done and the people I've hurt. I've done so many things wrong. Please forgive me!"

I don't know what I thought would happen. Nothing did. After a while I went back inside, laid down on the floor, pulled a blanket over my head and cried myself to sleep.

Then came New Year's Day!

When I woke up that morning, apart from the fact that my father had gone somewhere, everything was exactly the same – but everything had changed. The air was charged with some strange electricity I'd never felt before. I walked outside. Everything was in vivid color and coursing with life. And so was I. My whole being hummed with a sense of joy and a weight had been lifted from my soul. There was no other way to put it.

Suddenly, I wasn't worried and anxious. I was overwhelmed by a sense of well-being and I just knew that, somehow, everything was going to be okay. I didn't immediately make the connection that Jesus had entered my life. That night, I related my experience to Mr. Van, and he explained that what I'd experienced was salvation. He was right. All at once, overnight, I knew that I knew! God thoroughly carried me in those early years as a new Christian, and I had gotten the job.

It was as if I'd tasted coffee – or chocolate – for the first time, and I couldn't get enough of it. I read the Bible voraciously, beginning with the *Gospel of John* in the New Testament, as Mr. Van suggested. That's where I met Jesus, my Savior. I was like a sponge. One-by-one my fleshly desires – once so seductive and destructive – faded away and were replaced with activities that had Jesus at their center.

I started attending church regularly and eventually became a church teacher and speaker, youth group co-leader, young adult and college group co-leader, and I was the homeless outreach coordinator and leader with City Team Ministries, which wanted to bring me on board as a full time employee/minister. As a good part of my duties in that position would have been development and fundraising, for which I didn't feel the best fit, I declined. I also served as a counselor for troubled young adults through Star House Ministries.

The gentle conviction of the Scripture and the strength of the Holy Spirit helped free me from some of my bad habits. I began feeling close to the Lord. I even felt called to full-time ministry and, in time, went into ministry training.

However, just like after the first blush of a new romance, that initial passion waned and I began to associate with my old "friends," and soon, frustrated that my life hadn't suddenly and magically become perfect, wandered away from God and slipped back into those chains that had held me captive for so long.

During this time I became possessed by my former longing to become a member of the Special Forces. So now I was essentially living two lives, my Christian life – which had really become a facade – and my Army Reserves life in which I was aggressively pursuing my dream of becoming a Green Beret.

Through it all, my need to prove myself – to myself, my dad, and the world at large – hadn't diminished, it had just been sublimated to my obvious failures and, then, my newfound beliefs.

I regret, now, that no one in the Church questioned my motives, but that's not really fair. Everyone was supportive and encouraged my determination to serve my country. The fact is, and I knew at a subconscious level – my dreams were much more selfish than patriotic.

For the time being, I continued living between these three worlds, my old life, my new life, and the life of my military aspirations, and I was torn.

I still felt a strong calling to minister but seemed to encounter nothing but roadblocks in my Christian life. Work, a place to live, transportation, my health, church relationships – all of those things that everyone deals with every day were, for some reason, overwhelming for me. I felt all order and direction slipping away, but it was a gradual, subtle process – like ocean waves slowly eroding the foundation of a house built on sand.

Before long I was somewhere else in my heart and no longer starting every day at my Savior's feet. That gave temptation a foothold, and before long, it sprang up in full array. It came with the one old temptation I hadn't yet identified, the idol I had built of my pride. Equal parts ego, anger, and a touch of masochism all wrapped neatly in the flag this idol had it all. But it's feet were clay. They couldn't outrun the ghosts of my past – a platoon of phantoms led by my drunken, abusive father.

The echo of their voices haunted me. "You're a wimp! Lazy! Stupid! You'll always be a nobody!" Goaded by that spirit of pride, I determined to silence those voices by becoming tougher, harder, to form a thicker shell between myself and the world. I resolved that, whatever it took, I'd fulfill my dream of becoming a Green Beret, to become a hero in my own eyes, in the eyes of the world. How else would I ever be strong enough to beat back my father's shadow?

And so I took over my life again.

I justified my newfound determination by convincing myself that I'd originally misunderstood God's calling. Clearly, He was shutting so-called Christian doors in my life on purpose to show me my error. What I was doing, in fact – what I have often done since, and what I've seen many people do – is interpreting my own desires as God's will.

That's a dangerous game, so easy to play, but impossible to win. Nevertheless, for the time being, I made God my ventriloquist's doll, putting words in His mouth and, in that way, making Him give me permission to do whatever I darn well intended to do anyway.

Still, I knew that New Year's Eve something had happened. Something real, and I wasn't prepared to abandon Christianity altogether. Instead, semi-subconsciously, I just redefined it, forming a personal, private theology that conformed to the shape of my desires. I decided God was a lot more liberal than the conservatism I'd been introduced to. Since Jesus made wine, I could drink wine. He hung out with sinners, so I could hang out with sinners. They called him a glutton, so . . . well, you see the mindset I'd fallen into.

I went to parties and blended in seamlessly. I started believing I'd only narrowly escaped become a fundamental Christian extremist. I felt like God wanted me to live and pursue a life alternative to that one – that maybe He was more likely to be found outside the church – after all, Jesus spent most of his time among the ordinary people, out in the countryside and by the Sea of Galilee. Why couldn't he just as easily be found in the Army Special Forces?

After transferring and then graduating from San Jose State University with a bachelor's degree in Behavioral Science with a 3.01 GPA (.01 percent higher than my dad's ironically), I set out to become the Green Beret I'd always imagined was at the core of my being, eager to break out and prove himself.

That college degree was proof to the world, to those ghosts, to my father, that I was neither stupid nor lazy. Now I set out to prove I wasn't a wimp, either.

Chapter Nine

I was determined to qualify for the Special Forces, whatever it took. The first step was to interview with a Special Forces unit. The closest one at the time was in Novato, California, near San Francisco; a two hour drive north for me. My mother worked at a big insurance company at the time with someone who belonged to the unit; he happened to be the First Sergeant there, meaning he was in charge of all the enlisted soldiers. The only position above him in the unit was that of Sergeant Major. His name was Bruce and, due in no small part to my mother's connection, I was able to meet with him.

As a result of that meeting I secured an interview with the executive officer, who invited me to transfer my Reserve status to this unit (12th Special Forces Group). There, I was placed in the Intelligence section, which was more of an administrative position, but it was a foot in the door. As soon as I could, I requested admission into the training section, and was accepted.

This section was designed for those seeking to become Special Forces qualified and who wanted to serve on an Operational Detachment Alpha team (or ODA). These are twelve-man teams of infantry soldiers who are selected and trained to perform highly specialized covert clandestine operations behind enemy lines. This required infiltrating and exfiltrating in stealth either by parachuting into the target area or, if possible, underwater with SCUBA gear.

Once transferred to this training section, I had to prepare myself for the rigorous qualification and selection process in order to make it on one of these very elite Green Beret teams. Second, I had to pass a very thorough medical physical exam. You must be in top physical condition and possess no abnormalities or disabilities (no heart murmurs, bad eye sight, bad knees, etc). I then had to re-take the Armed Services Vocational Aptitude Battery test, better known as the ASVAB, which tests general education and will identify any vocation for which I might best be suited.

Special Forces requires a High Aptitude in general. Scoring high on the ASVAB in all areas - in the top ten or fifteen percent - is a must. The candidates most likely to be selected are highly intelligent, extroverted, Type-A personalities. They have to demonstrate the ability to learn fast, retain information, and exhibit initiative to a high degree.

The next requirement was Airborne Qualification, which I had already attained at the Army Paratrooper school at Fort Benning, Georgia in the summer of 1988. Candidates also had to be a non-commissioned officer or rank of at least E-5 (sergeant) with prior years of service on active duty. Check another box. Then I had to pass a PT test, physical fitness test, with at least 280 points out of a possible maximum of 300. Typically, this meant I had to be able to run two miles in under thirteen minutes, do eighty push-ups in two minutes and seventy-five sit-ups in two minutes, all back to back.

Meantime, I had to pass an intensive background investigation. Although legal infractions could be disqualifying, more important was whether or not I could be deemed a threat to national security. Did my psychological profile suggest someone who, under threat or inducement, might sell secrets or whose activities might make me susceptible to blackmail or seduction?

Trust is everything in the Special Forces and, since trust is built on truthfulness, at this stage you confess your darkest secrets, hold nothing back. It's a humbling experience but, like ten minutes in the confessional, cleansing.

Attending Special Forces Selection

As part of the Special Forces Assessment and Selection routine, SFAS, we filed into the Fort Bragg auditorium at 9:00 - two-hundred and eighty soldiers formed row upon row - wearing our fatigues. We stood at ease.

All name tags and unit identification were stripped from our clothing. The only thing by which we could be identified was a hastily sewn strip of cloth above the right top pocket which bared the markings of our new identification. With black indelible ink, I had written the number "76." I was no longer a soldier in training, but, rather, a number being evaluated. For three weeks, this was who I was. The hall remained silent. After a few moments, an order was called out.

"Attention!"

To the podium strolled the Colonel in charge of the Special Forces Assessment and Selection; in his green beret and starched fatigues, he looked at all faces before him. "Take your seats, men," he said casually.

We sat in unison.

"Welcome to SFAS, men. For the next three weeks, you will be evaluated on your performance. Since you are meeting with me here today, it means you have met several demanding prerequisites. Congratulations. It's a start."

He slowly paced the stage. "Roughly sixty-five to seventy percent of you won't make it. SFAS is designed to seek out the soldiers with the type of character most epitomizing the Green Beret. No matter what, you are all undoubtedly fine soldiers. Perhaps, though, not the type we are looking for.

"As you may have noticed in your welcome packets there is a lack of specific criteria given for this course. It is our mission to see how you will react in any given combat situation. To do this, you will enter an environment that simulates actual combat. Therefore, as is most often the case in combat, you won't be given a schedule of events. You will, however, be deprived of sleep, food, and shelter. We will push your body's endurance levels to the utmost extremes. You will spend many hours alone. We want to see what makes you tick. We want to take the wrapping off and see what's inside.

"In this next three weeks, we will find out who you really are. We will know you better than you know yourselves. This process is not one-hundred-percent fool proof, but it's dang close. No one's going to help you. You will be forced to rely on yourselves. Men, if it was easy, we wouldn't be the Special Forces, would we?"

He paused, then stopped and surveyed our frozen faces. Looking us over for a moment, he continued.

"Look to your left and look to your right. Chances are that man won't be with you three weeks from now. You have come here from all different walks of life. Not by fate, but by choice. You all have your own individual reasons for wanting to be here. Some of you *don't* want to be here, you just don't know it yet. And after you have given everything you've got, finding you can go no further, the man that reaches deep down into his soul pulling out the source which keeps his desires burning is the man who will be able to complete the mission. These are the men we want in Special Forces - ones willing to go the distance, no matter what. Good luck, men."

"On your feet!" a voice cried out as the Colonel swiftly made an exit. We slowly filed out. By 0500 hours the next morning, everyone was at the training field. It was a cold February morning at Fort Bragg, North Carolina. In the early morning darkness, the stadium was lit with overhead lights. Our breath condensed into an eerie fog.

In what appeared to be carefully-orchestrated chaos,

we stood in columns waiting our turn. A physical fitness test was being administered. Two-hundred and eighty points must be accumulated, and I was not looking so good. Wearing my Army gray sweats and red-numbered 76 bib, I vigorously pushed at the earth.

"One! One! One! Soldier, your chest must make contact with the ground. One! One! Lock those elbows. Three! Three! Back straight! Back straight! Six! Seven! Eight!" Desperately attempting my best push-ups, a Green Beret evaluator kneeling next to me counted only the perfect ones.

My arms were moving like pistons as I started to get into an even rhythm. The column of troops behind me looked on as the grader then counted each of my push-ups. I had to do as many as I could in two minutes.

"You have fifteen seconds remaining. Sixty-seven! Sixty-eight!"

I forced my exhausted arms to push once more. "Sixty-nine and seventy! Time!"

I stood. My arms felt like rubber and my head pounded. I moved to the back of the line to wait my next turn. The evaluator hadn't counted at least twenty of my push-ups and that bothered me. I wondered why. In all the time I had been in the Army, with all the PT tests I had taken along the way, I never produced a bad push-up. Well, at least, not until then.

I had three more events to finish: sit-ups for two minutes, a two-mile timed run, and a fifty-meter swim test in fatigues and boots.

The other guys were faring about the same. They were being shorted. Occasionally, a candidate complained as he continued the exercise. If they didn't pass, they went home.

I was in good condition and I knew it. I had trained for months for this. And now I was being cheated. Again, I did my sit-ups, but only sixty-two of them counted.

The two-mile run was next.

As we finished the push-ups and sit-ups, we headed to the quarter-mile track where we jumped up and down trying to stay warm. Our taller, lengthier marathon-types stretched for the record times they were going to set. It looked like the Olympic tryouts.

Our massive group of soldiers was split into three sections. I stood at the starting line with the first bunch. The narrow track was stuffed with runners. As I stood at the ready, I wondered how they could cheat me on this event.

"Go!" barked the evaluator with the stopwatch.

Us runners sprang from the starting line. Two miles equals eight laps around the track. I would have choked up a lung to get a 12:45 minute time. I stayed close to the inside as I rounded the first corner. Other runners with their bibs flying in the wind, bumped off one another as we all tried to stay to the inside. Gravel was flying in every direction. I rounded my first lap.

"1:25!" the evaluator shouted.

We started to spread out. I went into my own world. I heard only the pounding of my own heart and saw my hands rocketing up and down. My concentration sent me even deeper. The once-thundering storm of runners around me became a muffled whisper. I turned another lap.

"3:01!"

My breath was heavy and fast. Streams of sweat fell into my eyes burning them. "Push! Push! Come on . . .!" I grunted to myself.

I thought back to those push-ups and sit-ups the evaluator hadn't counted. My arms pumped faster. A burning sensation gripped my lungs. My legs ached for oxygen. I pushed harder with but one thought. "Faster! Faster!"

"5:09!"

My heart raced, feeling as if it would explode. I made

another lap, then another. Stretching it out, I passed other runners.

"11:58!"

My final lap.

I gasped for air, but there was none. My arms, legs, and calves screamed out in pain threatening to stop me in my tracks. As if each stride was my last, I stretched. Blood from my lungs rose to my throat.

No air! No air! Like pure salt in my eyes, the sweat burned. Rounding another turn, the blood pounded in my head. The last turn.

Go! Go! Go! my mind commanded. *I need air! I need air!* my body screamed. I ignored it.

"12:47! 48! 49! Time!"

I stumbled past the evaluator who clicked the stopwatch. Unable to catch my breath, with my hands on my hips, I stumbled about as my legs and lungs fought to catch up.

As quickly as they left me, the sights and sounds around me returned. My survivor state of mind was gone. I knew I'd done well, but I wasn't sure how I'd scored on the push-ups and sit-ups.

My heart rate returned to normal and my breathing eased. Candidates all around me were busy recovering. Some just stood with their heads hanging. Others lay on the ground, sending deep breathes steaming into the crisp February morning. Some were throwing up and others, red-faced, paced back and forth.

We had given it our all. Runners continued to cross the finish line. I found myself thinking about the next event. I took a deep breath and looked skyward. The sun was beginning to rise and in the bright stadium lights I observed the insects colliding off one another as they fought for the heat and light.

Swim Test – Olympic Pool

Later at the swim test: Drip! Drip! Drip! Water streamed from my fatigues down my trouser legs and into my boots. At the edge of the long indoor pool, following a quick, cold rinsing, we all stood waiting our turn. Eight at a time, in our heavy fatigues and boots, we were to swim the length of the pool and back again. Evaluators stood on the sides with lifeguard poles at the ready. One kid from the first group got about half-way on the first leg and was struggling desperately to keep his head above water. He started to panic, thrashing frantically, but getting nowhere.

The rest of us, spread around the pool, shouted encouragement at him. "Come on! Come on! You can do it!" The sound echoed throughout the cavernous room.

"Shut up! Shut up!" yelled the evaluator over our cheers. "There will be no assistance given. Leave him alone!"

Everything went silent and only the swimmer's desperate attempts to get air, and the mad splashing of water could be heard. The kid tired and finally began to sink for the last time. His last outstretched hand slowly went under. The atmosphere was tense and the lifeguards waited.

Until the last possible moment, they waited.

Finally, one of them casually sent his long pole after the drowning candidate. Grabbing the end, the kid burst to the surface gasping for air. The pole was brought in and the candidate crawled onto the edge of the pool, exhausted.

He was gone and I knew it. Just like that. Although I was a great swimmer, I could not help but worry. The evaluator pointed to the next group of us and I jumped in the pool. Holding on to the edge of the pool, I could feel the weight and drag of my fatigues.

The evaluator stood at the end of the diving board and said, "Release."

I let go and started to kick and use my arms to stay

afloat. The Evaluator first checked for coherency in the eyes of each man. After a moment, feeling satisfied of this, he said, "Begin!"

I remained calm. In fact, I felt quite confident. I breast-stroked to the end of the pool, and without touching the edge, turned around. As I swam, I took long controlled stokes sending my body purposefully gliding under water. I raised my head and grabbed some more air. Even with the boots and fatigues, I swam easily.

Next to me, a soldier was struggling horribly. Wild-eyed with terror, his eyes met mine. He grabbed at me frantically to hold on and I was halted. Once again, our eyes met. I understood that look of desperation. I had seen it before in another man's eyes: my father's.

For a moment, I hesitated. For an instant, I was frozen.

Then I gripped the soldier's hand and ripped it off my arm. With one kick, I glided away leaving him sinking behind me. I got to the end of the pool.

The evaluator checked for coherency again. He gave me a thumbs-out of the pool. As I looked behind me, I saw the soldier kneeling at the edge of the pool coughing up water. Long strands of saliva hung from his mouth.

He turned his head and looked at me. I stood looking back for a moment, then turned away. A couple of guys patted me on the back as I walked by. Nothing would ever be said about performances during the three weeks at SFAS.

The Compound – Camp Mackall

The next day after the rest of the prerequisites were complete, we were transported out of Fort Bragg in the back of deuce and a half trucks, the canvas overhead snapping and slapping crisp salutes to the wintry wind. We gripped our collars tightly under our chins. It had begun to rain and the wheels kicked up a fine spray that settled on us in the back of the truck.

Facing me from his bench seat, number Ninety-eight watched me. With brown hair, a dark mustache, and dark green eyes, he stared. Although a couple of years older than me, his weight and build were about the same as mine. He leaned back in the bench seat and put a boot up on a rucksack.

"Hey! Seventy-six!"

"Yeah?" I said looking him in the eye.

"That boy almost took you down yesterday."

"Yep."

"You were pretty lucky, I figure."

I sat erect, suddenly feeling challenged.

"Oh? How do you figure?"

Ninety-eight looked out the back of the truck. "I don't know, but I think you do." He looked back at me. "Maybe, don't get so close to others, ya know?"

I nodded my head and looked down the road. After a lengthy pause, I said, "This ain't combat, candidate."

"Ain't it?" number Ninety-eight replied.

I glared at him a bit.

Ninety-eight shrugged. "Hey, I just thought I'd try and help out a little," he said with a grin.

I grinned back.

The big troop carrier bumped along the highway. Camp Mackall was about an hour-and-a-half away. The countryside foliage had become more and more dense. With vegetation of all sorts, we crossed over one long rolling hill after another.

Short, woody pine trees made up much of the landscape. The gates to the small compound opened as our convoy approached. Camp Mackall was isolated from most soldiers and sat alone amidst the dense North Carolina landscape. As the rain continued to pour, I spied rows of crudely built troop huts. A tall cyclone fence with rolling strands of concertina wire encircled the compound.

Like some primitive special operations base camp, Camp Mackall fitted the bare necessities image perfectly. Clothes hung on lines despite the drenching rain. Three spigots rose from the ground and tin wash pans laid about. Mostly sand and gravel covered the ground with an occasional crop of weeds. To one corner of the compound, sat a row of old Jeeps and trailers.

Although the camp seemed primitive and somewhat deserted, I felt it also possessed a sense of purpose.

The trucks came to a stop in the middle of the compound and the tailgates dropped. We began to off-load. I jumped off the truck with my gear. It took mere seconds for the ice-cold rain to drench me. We moved quickly, and there was shouting to get organized. I picked up my gear and started moving toward what I thought to be the formation area.

A couple of guys shouted, "Formation! Formation!"

An evaluator came out of the head shed and slowly walked to the front of us. Seemingly unaware of the rain, he walked up smiling.

"Welcome to Camp Mackall Special Forces Assessment and Selection Facility. This is really easy, Guys. You have a chalkboard on that tree over there," he pointed. "Everything you need to know will be written on it. You will check it as many times as you have to. No one will remind you of anything. That board is your instructions. Follow them to the letter. Pay attention to detail. Do not miss anything. Do not ask any of the evaluators or cadre any questions.

"We are not here to lead you or supervise you. We are not here to train you or advise you. It's all up to you. We are here to just simply monitor and evaluate you. If you get injured, if you are ill, if you become a heat casualty, or hypothermic, you can see a medic. If you need further medical assistance, you are not gonna get it here. You will have to VW, "voluntarily withdrawal" from Selection. We only provide basic first aid here.

"If you want to finish, you're just gonna have to suck it up and drive on. Your rack time will be limited. Sleep is not a luxury you can afford here. You will be issued one MRE, "Meals Ready-to-Eat," a day. Do not let fatigue and the lack of supervision get the best of you. Never deviate from basic soldiering rules and regulations. We see a lot of guys get tired and forget.

"If you leave your weapon, if you are more than an arm's length away from it, you are wrong. No one is going to correct you. If it is seen happening, it will be written up with your roster number. To put this in terms you can all understand, if you are late, if you cheat, if you lie, if you lose anything, if you make a mistake, if you run out of water, if you do not follow the instructions on the board exactly, you most likely will not be selected come selection day. It pays to be a winner here.

"We are an equal opportunity employer though. We give you as much slack as you need to fail or succeed."

He paused and looked out into the ranks as the rain still poured. "And some of you don't want to be here. You just don't know it yet."

Finishing his speech, he wasted no time. "Now, fall out and pick up your meal which is in the box." He pointed to a large cardboard box of MRE's. "Move out to your assigned huts. Check the board at 1900 hours for your first instructions. Move out!"

In my new hut, I found ten bunk beds. Five to each side. It was barren except for the cold cement floor and the mattressless steel bunk frames.

I moved to an empty bunk and began to organize my equipment. I rolled my sleeping bag down the length of the bunk. I looked around and saw guys checking the springs. No one complained. This is part of what we were being tested on: our ability to deal with the lack of comfort.

I laid gingerly on my bunk testing its comfort. There was none, just squeaky springs sticking in my back. The job of SFAS was to make you feel as uncomfortable as possible all the time.

Can we take it? That's what it came down to. After a while, the ones that could not would eventually blow a fuse and end up quitting. This suited me just fine. I wanted to see each man tested. If they could not take it, then good. They did not belong, and Special Forces would get only the best.

A short thin Italian kid was lying in the bunk next to me. His blood shot eyes bulged and his rough five o' clock shadow gave him a sloppy, unkempt appearance. Soaked to the bone with his hands behind his head, he stared at the bunk springs above him.

"It's cold ain't it?" he said in a thick New Jersey accent.

I looked around and figured he must have been talking to me, so I shrugged. "It's supposed to be."

"Yeah, guess so. Albert. Nice to meet you, okay?" He extended a hand to shake mine.

"Don." I shook his hand. Then we both settled back into our bunks.

"You seventy-six? I'm roster number one-hundred. It's a good number to have, I think. Lucky, you know?"

"Strong number, Albert."

"Kind of high profile though. Don't know if I like that."

"You a little nervous, Albert?"

"Who me? I don't think so." A pause. "Well, maybe a little." He held up a couple fingers showing about an inch between. A long pause followed, and we just stared at the springs above us. "Ya know, a lot of guys don't make it."

"That's what they tell me," I replied.

Another pause. "I got to make it, man. You never hear what happens out here, though."

"What do you mean?" I said feeling a bit more interested.

"What? You ain't heard?"

"No."

"They got boys dyin' out here. A candidate died of heat stroke last cycle. In January, no less. Man, it happens all the time. Boys be walkin' around with both lungs full of pneumonia, and then drop somewhere out there."

"I never heard, but I guess anything's possible."

Albert, somewhat worked up then, continued. "I mean, they let you *die* out here!" Another pause.

"You got to want it," I said softly and as if to myself. Another pause.

"They're gonna try and hurt us, Don."

"Yeah, I know. But this is just something I need to do."

"You mean prove?"

"No," I said. "Do!"

Albert shrugged. "If you say so."

"Let me give you some advice, Albert. Don't let them break you. Play the game, be what they're looking for. Survivor-type, you know?"

"Survivin's one thing. Dyin's another."

A candidate walked by with his sleeping bag draped over his shoulder.

"Better not get caught lying in those racks."

Albert and I flew up and out of our bunks.

Chapter Ten

The Obstacle Course

Early the next morning was cool and crisp. The rain had stopped, and the clouds disappeared sometime the night before. With a fresh new day at hand, Selection Phase was underway. The one-and-a-half-mile obstacle course waited.

In the woods behind the compound, odd structures were sprawled about. We two hundred some odd candidates were following Green Berets who were giving us walk-throughs.

"This obstacle is called the 'Dirty Name.' You must maneuver over the first horizontal log, jump to the second higher one and then to the third, flip over the top, then down to the ground. Then move out quickly to the next obstacle." We walked to the next one.

"This is the 'Leg Breaker.' Any questions?"

Six ropes ascended sixty feet, tied to a horizontal log. Other ropes descended from the log at an arching angle back to the ground. As the exhausted candidates reached the top of the first rope, many fall trying to switch to the second rope. A fitting nickname because of the injuries it caused. We moved to the next obstacle.

"This is the 'Executioner.'" A rope ascended twenty feet to a horizontal log. We had to climb the rope, flip on top of the log, stand up and step over to another log. From there another log rose at an angle, extending the over-all height another fifteen feet. The log thinned drastically as it rose. From there, a rickety ladder was fastened horizontally and we had to walk across the rungs. That rose another ten feet. A rope hung horizontally at the other end. We had to maneuver along that rope to another rope which drops to the ground.

"This over here is called the 'Buster!' And with the rain yesterday, these logs are as slick as snot."

Long telephone poles rose at an angle towards each other forming a triangle. At about twenty feet up they met one another. As we ran up the log, the width thinned out, making it virtually impossible to make the switch to the adjoining one. It could be a painful and costly slip.

We were taken through the rest of the obstacle course, being shown obstacles with names like the "Terminator," "Dead Man's Jump," "Spine Tingler," "Charlotte's Web," and the "Back-Breaker."

The grotesque tour took an hour. Ropes, nets, logs, and ditches were in every direction, around every corner. For what should have been a simple test of confidence and coordination, a lot of medical vehicles seemed to be present.

I found my place in line; red bibs bearing our roster numbers showed brightly against our dark fatigues. My heart started to pound with anticipation. I thought about the slick logs and obstacles like the "Leg Breaker."

The evaluator clicked his stopwatch and moved the first man through.

"Go!"

At one-minute intervals, we were released onto the course. As the line moved along, I started shaking my legs and arms out. The closer I got to the start line, the more I withdrew into my own world. All the sights and sounds around me began to vanish until I was alone in my own world of survival. I got to the front of the line.

"Roster Number Seventy-six, go!"

I dashed past the evaluator under the watchful eyes of the candidates awaiting their turn. I quickly high-stepped the first thirty hurdles. A man to my right slipped and fell. I moved on, running as fast as I could around a corner and jumped onto the monkey bars. I swung rung by rung. About halfway I slipped off. There was grease on the bar. I ran back to the start, picked up some dirt and rubbed it into my hands. An evaluator wrote something in his notebook.

I power-gripped each rung as I rocketed to the other side. Already winded, I hopped from log to log on the next obstacle, leap-frogging across.

I darted to the "Leg Breaker." I watched a candidate crash to the ground screaming in pain. An evaluator stood over him and calmly asked if he wanted to attempt the obstacle again.

I leapt onto the rope and, hand over hand, climbed to the top. Another candidate to my right went sliding down the rope burning his hands. Hands aching with pain, I lunged for the cross-over rope and swung my legs onto it. I slid as quickly as I could to the bottom. I looked at the evaluator, who waved me on.

Sweat rolled down my face and into my eyes as I charged to the next obstacle. Another rope rose fifty feet straight up. Men stood hunched over trying to catch their breath. I leapt, wrapping my feet to get more pulling power and pulled, hand over hand. I could not get up.

I looked at the evaluator, exhausted.

"Will you be attempting this obstacle again?" he's asked.

I looked at the other soldiers' failing attempts and said, "No!"

"Move out, Seventy-six!"

I ran to the next rope. A candidate stood frozen on "The Executioner's" ladder. I grabbed the rope.

A soldier flew down past me. He bounced hard off a log and crashed to the ground. I heard the snap of his arm when it broke. The medics sat on the hood of their ambulances watching.

I pulled myself over the log. Breathing heavy, I started feeling dizzy. I skirted to the adjoining log and ascended to the top. With my arms outstretched, I maintained my balance. I looked down and, putting one shaky foot in front of the other, crossed the ladder and slid down the rope to the bottom.

I stumbled, fell to the ground then got up.

I bolted to the next obstacle and slid onto the ground on my stomach, slithered into a ditch under foot-high barbed wire and worked my way through and out.

A Green Beret was standing in the woods observing me. I rolled to my feet and wiped some blood from my forehead, smearing it across my face.

I swallowed hard and ran as fast as I could to gain momentum barely making the thinning top of the "Buster" log. I paused long enough to regain some balance and ran down the other side.

I was winded and my head was pounding. Every bone ached. I felt bruised and scratched from head to toe. I jumped on to the "Dirty Name" and quickly slid off. I tried again. I made it up, gained my balance, and leaped to the next parallel log. At about fifteen feet above the ground, I slowly stood on the thin bark-stripped pole. As I started to lose my balance, I jumped to the high parallel log and rolled over the other side, dropped crashing to the bottom and rolled onto my feet.

The evaluator lethargically waved me on.

Scrambling over the barbed wire mounds, I made my way to the cargo netting called "Charlotte's Web" because of the soldiers it had captured and entangled. I followed the guy in front of me up the sixty-foot monstrosity. One after the other, we grabbed the woven ropes and vigorously pulled ourselves over the top and went tumbling down the other side.

He sprang to his feet and took off running, and I was right on his heels. I didn't know what was keeping me going. Into a tunnel, we barreled as fast as we could. Soldier's screams and shouts echoed in the chambers. In the darkness, I tried to feel my way. I crawled on my hands and knees and, after coming to an intersection I turned right.

A panicked candidate tore at me, screaming and angry. I moved by. I took a left and crawled some more. Around the dark corner, I saw some light and moved towards it. As I reached the opening, I grabbed the rope and climbed out. My eyes ached from the brightness. I felt disoriented but started running anyway.

I made it through the "Pit of darkness," a series of tunnels with any number of ways out. For some, it was the *pit of their greatest fears*. I was determined it wouldn't claim me. Soaked with sweat, my face and fatigues caked with dirt and grime, I ran blindly. My knees and elbows bled, as did my face from the cut I'd gotten from the barbed wire. I jogged my tired and beaten body to the next obstacle.

Candidates were strewn all around. Ambulance sirens could be heard. Some soldiers sat off to the side, too exhausted to continue. I stumbled and weaved by them. In front of me, the "Spine Tingler" awaited.

An evaluator sat on a log and smiled at me. I knew what he was thinking, and I was not about to give him the satisfaction of being right. Logs paralleled each other, as they rose to form a huge triangle. I moved onto the obstacle, completely exhausted.

As I began to weave my body through the logs, I saw they were smeared with blood. I grunted and pulled, contorting by body to slip through the narrow openings. My spine screamed with sharp pain as I manipulated my body through the obstacle.

Nothing was going to stop me. Something inside me had taken over and I was not going to give up. Knowing that I was disappointing the sadistic evaluator, I got through the obstacle and spat on the ground. I had beaten the trap. The evaluator scratched his chin and half-heartedly waved me on.

Dragging with each step and unable to get enough air, I

pumped, pushed, and climbed my way over more obstacles. I lost sight of others somewhere back at the "Spine Tingler." At that point, I did not care where anyone was. I just wanted to finish.

More tired than I could ever remember being, I saw nothing but my boots dragging on the ground to the next obstacle. I made a final lunge for what I can only have guessed to be another rope. I swung clear of a ditch full of water below me and rolled onto the ground to a stop.

"Time! Roster Number Seventy-six!"

I had crossed the finish line.

Cross Country Run

24 hours later I was running a trail cross-country through pounding rain. My boots slammed into puddles of water as I made my way down the fire break. Lush vegetation rose from either side of the trail. Another candidate was ahead in the distance. I followed him

Deep sand slowed my stride. I continued to wipe the water from my face. I could see my breath and my hands were red from the numbing cold. With only the sound of rain and my breathing for company, I ran silently and alone. Candidates ran behind and in front of me, up the hills and down around the bends through the meadows.

I followed the marks of red tape streamers. With each stride, I landed carefully. I did not want to twist my ankle. Somewhere ahead, someone fast was setting the pace. I thought about the obstacle course and its sheer madness.

The evaluators were looking for something more than coordination. They were looking to see how we dealt with pain. For a week they had pushed us without mercy, perhaps too far.

Men were becoming ill. Wounds were getting infected, and tempers were flaring. Throughout the daily formations, I watched our numbers dwindle to one-hundred and seventy. Candidates had quit in the night or became too sick or injured to go on. The men remaining were in it for the long haul.

I knew that everyone left just wanted to finish the course. It was a personal challenge, something different for everyone; something no one had to understand, just respect. Broken feet, infected blisters, or sickness - these men ignored them all.

It's just an understanding. People will die trying to finish, if they must. It's a personal quest where physical trauma is not of any significance. There's something deeper at stake, something almost spiritual.

As a man's body starts to collapse, something else takes over. Something was driving us beyond our physical limitations. I pictured my father in the public storage yard where he lived for a while. I envisioned my childhood and how he always thought the worst of me. That was a sufficiently powerful incentive to keep me going.

Cresting the last hill, I saw the finish line in the distance. My swollen ankles sent dull pain up my legs, but I would not be stopped. I passed runners who wobbled on the verge of the road, stumbling like zombies from *Night of the Living Dead*. Another one stumbled and fell; I lengthened my stride, leaving them all behind.

Back at the Hut

Halfway through our three weeks, Albert sat on the edge of his bunk. The day's events were complete. Up until then, we had covered one hundred and twenty miles. Through the door, we staggered in from the darkness and each of us slowly limped to our bunks. The atmosphere was somber as we licked our wounds.

Like a hospital ward, limping candidates wandered from bunk to bunk. I was busy repacking my gear. Albert gingerly untied one of his boot laces. Painfully he removed the well-worn boot and saw a mangled and twisted sock soaked with blood.

He slowly peeled it from his foot and flaps of skin tore off as he pulled. He bit his lower lip. With the sock removed, his eyes filled with tears of pain. The entire foot looked like it has been stripped of skin. Deep infected blisters surrounded the raw tissue. He groaned.

"That's got to smart," I said tightening up a strap on my rucksack.

"What am I gonna do?"

I shrugged my shoulders. I had no good ideas for Albert's feet. My helping other people did not usually turn out so good.

Albert propped his foot on top of his muddy boot, "This ruck is killing me. I can't walk anymore." Fear came over him as he stared at his mangled foot. "You got to help me, Don"

I looked into eyes of desperation for a moment. "I don't godda do anything, Al!"

"Look at this man! Look at it. . ." he moaned, tossing his bloody sock into the corner.

"I see it," I said. "But I have no idea what we can do that will make it any better."

"Really?" Albert asked me. "How bad is it? Is it as bad as it feels?"

I was careful not to show anything on my face. "It's not good, Al. It doesn't look good at all."

"That's all you got to say?" Albert said, with tears still in his eyes.

"Yes."

Albert couldn't move, but he was mad. "For almost two weeks you've been parading around here like you don't care. I don't know why your feet ain't messed up, but look around."

"Why?"

"It's just not me, Don. It's everybody. It's all of us!"

I looked around and I knew how bad everyone was hurting. But I could only help myself. I looked back at Albert but said nothing.

Before he could reply, one of the Green Berets walked through the door.

"All right. Listen up! First call has been changed from 0200 hours to 0600 hours. You're gonna get eight hours tonight. You better make good use of it and hit those racks. Lights out in fifteen minutes." He looked down at his feet. "Somebody wipe this blood up off my floor. I might slip and kill myself."

After the sergeant turned and walked out, I grabbed my bag and headed for the latrine. Inside I found an empty stall. I looked around to see if anyone was watching and then closed the door behind me. I sat on the toilet and unlaced my boots. I pulled my bag near. I took off my first boot, then my second.

Sitting, I stared down and saw two blood-soaked socks. I ignored the bile rising in my stomach and quickly removed my socks. I did not have the luxury of emotions which did not help anyway.

My feet were bloody and swollen, looking almost as bad as Albert's. An entire toenail dangled freely off the side of my big toe. Both heels looked like chunks had been carved from them and blisters the size of silver dollars oozed thick dark fluid. Opening my bag, I reached in. I pulled out a clean moist rag and scrubbed my feet. I used some soap and wiped my feet clean, all the while biting on the inside of my cheek until I tasted blood. I put on another pair of socks and quickly pulled my boots back on.

Standing up, I removed my shirt and tried to blot the raw skin on the small of my back and shoulders where the rucksack straps and padding had rubbed the skin to raw flesh. I put my shirt back on and stuffed the blood-soaked rag back into my bag.

I heard a door open and someone slowly walking by. Looking underneath the stall walls, I saw boots. The man walked to the end and back again. I saw the boots stop in front of my stall. After a moment, the boots walked away and out the door. I gave a sigh of relief, collected my gear and left the latrine.

Outside, standing in the shadows, I heard, "You know what they say?"

I stopped in my tracks. The first sergeant was standing in the dark, leaning against the wall. An eerie glow was caste from his smoldering cigarette.

"They say that pain is nothing more than weakness escaping the body. Do you believe that?"

I said, "Yeah. I guess I do."

The first sergeant said, "Do, do, do. To do, to do, or not to do. What to do? I don't know, but I think circles are round, boxes are square, and you are who you are, no matter what the pain may say."

I looked out the side of my eye at him for a moment. His cigarette discarded and hands cupped to his eyes, he continued.

"I see many assorted soldiers in uniform. Some bigger. Some smaller. But they're all soldiers. And the thing is, they want me to see the difference."

He dropped his hands and looked at me. "How can I see the difference? Maybe if I just use the same old, tired grading matrixes and stopwatch, I'll learn everything I need to know. Somehow though, I don't think so."

He held a finger up. "I know. I'll throw away the stopwatch and let you all show me who you are - really. Surely, I will see the differences then. You're bound to show me the real you eventually. I've got nothin' but time."

The first sergeant slowly backed away and out of sight until his words were hanging on the breeze. "We'll see who you really are. I think we are both gonna be surprised. Actually, Seventy-six, you're an open book and you don't even know it."

Kind of spooky, and a little over the top. Life had become like a Hollywood script. But what are you gonna do? Back at the hut a few minutes later, I packed my kit in silence.

"You get lost out there?" Albert asked.

"Nope."

"We get eight hours rack time tonight."

I did not reply.

"Don, you all right?"

I thought about that question. I did not know the answer, but it did not really matter.

"Just fine," I answered softly.

Land Navigation Test

At exactly 0200-hours, explosions rocked the compound. Green Berets walked around the huts tossing grenade simulators. In the darkness, we all responded in chaos.

"Let's go, sleeping beauties. It's time to go to work. Form it up outside. Let's go!"

"I thought they were going to let us sleep!" Albert groaned.

"Change of plans, I guess," I said, picking up my gear and moving outside.

Albert sat on his bunk for a moment looking bewildered. He watched everyone walk by. He grabbed his pillow and threw it against the wall. "Great."

Outside in the darkness, my ears were still ringing from the simulators. Smoke swirled gently, rising up and ghosted away. Men moved swiftly from every direction going to formation. Barely visible, I watched silhouettes move by. The air was cold and damp. I could feel it cutting right through me. I quickly put my thirty-pound web belt with suspenders on. Canteens, butt pack, ammo pouches, and navigation equipment made up my personal gear.

In my right thigh pocket a map was folded into a zip lock bag. A compass hung off my shoulder strap and was stuffed inside my fatigue shirt. I picked up the corners of my sixty-five-pound ruck at the frame. I lifted the rucksack up and over and slid it down the other side of my back. With two quick tugs, I pulled the shoulder straps tight over my wounds, careful not to wince with the pain. Making my way over to formation, I found my place.

Number One Hundred, Albert, slowly and painfully limped to his place behind me. To my left and down a few men, I spotted Number Ninety-eight. His rucksack hung tightly packed and he wore his hat with the brim low over his eyebrows. He stood poised and strong. I was impressed by the image I saw silhouetted in the darkness. I could sense his confidence and I respected that.

A figure walked in front of the formation as we rocked from side to side trying to stay warm.

"Alright, listen up! Rack time is over, and in the future I suggest you get moving a lot faster." He raised his hand. "Who here really thought we were gonna let you guys sleep all night?" No one raised their hands. He paused to stare holes in us for a few seconds. "We've still got another week and you already look like something the dog threw up."

Indeed, the ranks of men were worn and beaten. The lack of sleep and food was taking its toll. Our uniforms were torn and hastily sewn and patched. Like rag dolls, with sunken eyes and scratched faces, we stood, though some just barely. We had covered hundreds of miles on foot. Over hills, through woods and streams, and across valleys, we had pushed ourselves to beat the stopwatch at every turn.

"There are one-hundred and forty-two of you left. At this rate, there will be nobody here come next week."

Candidates were dropping like flies. Broken legs, concussions, heat exhaustion, hypothermia, and sickness plagued many of us. And even though many of us wanted to continue, our bodies were giving up on us. Like Albert, other men stood in the ranks with injuries that required attention.

I looked down at the boot of the man standing next to me; he hadn't bothered trying to lace it. A piece of duct tape was fastened around the top holding it together. His ankle was obviously broken. He stared ahead like a zombie.

"Tonight's mission is a ten-hour land navigation exercise. You must successfully navigate to four locations. At each point, you will be given a new set of coordinates. There will be no use of flashlights except to plot your routes on your map. You will talk to no one. This is not a team event. You must navigate as individuals. You will be spread out over sixty miles of terrain. If you should become a casualty, activate your starburst flare. Make sure it clears the tress, gentlemen, because you only have one. Stay at that location and we'll find you . . . eventually. Now, move out to your designated deuce and a halfs."

Eight trucks cranked up their cold diesel engines. Freezing wind whipped through the Deuce and a Half's truck bed. The front canvass section was missing. Candidates huddled down close to their knees. Number Ninety-eight cracked a light stick in the darkness, the eerie green illuminated his face. I watched him, and then our eyes met. He smirked.

After traveling an hour, the trucks came to a stop in some desolate location where two sand roads intersected amongst the heavy wood line. I jumped off and found a spot on the ground to lay out my map. On my knees, I closely studied the map by red-lensed flashlight. I placed a finger at my current location, and with my other hand I ran a finger up the map to the location I believed to be my first navigation point.

Suddenly another candidate started ranting and raving. "That's it! That is it!"

I just looked at him.

"I can't take this anymore!" In the dark his silhouette paced back and forth ripping up his map.

"Get me out of this frozen wasteland. You people are crazy! You're all out of your minds!"

A Green Beret approached him and quietly walked him away. I turned off my flashlight and then stuffed my map into my shirt. I looked out into the night, seeing only ghostly shadows of my surroundings. I opened my compass, and fluorescent light shot out. I took a reading then looked down at my pace count* beads and pushed them to the top of the string.

I took off at a run disappearing into the darkness. After an hour or two traversing the sand roads and trails, beneath my breath, I counted out my pace.

"Seventy-five, seventy-six, seventy-seven, . . . six-hundred." I stopped, pulled another bead down and looked around. Pulling my map out and using the light from my compass to check my location, I pointed to an intersection on the map, then looked around. Suddenly, I heard footsteps. A candidate came into view from the opposite direction. Passing by, he stomped his boot down twice. I watched him fade away. I took off again.

Further on another two hundred meters, I counted, "Seventy-four, seventy-five, seventy-six, seventy-seven . . . eight-hundred." I stopped, and in the darkness, looked around, checking my map again.

Refolding it and stuffing it away, I muttered, "Too far. I'm too far." I battled down my frustration.

I lowered to a knee and took some water from my canteen. Looking up, I saw the clouds part, revealing a bright moon. To my immediate right, an intersection slowly took shape as my eyes adjusted to the night.

"That's it. It's right there." I put my canteen away, pointing my compass, and took off up the road.

The forest was closing in. The trail was narrow and uneven. Running, walking, breathing heavily—counting my pace—the narrowing trail turned me left and right. I walked slower, brushed by tree limbs and bushes until, finally, I halted, unable to go any further. In the darkness, I stood, listening. I recognized the sound of a stream. Taking a few more steps, I felt my boots starting to fill with water. Then a little further, although I could not see it, I was halted by a fallen log. Trying to look from left to right, I imagined I was trapped, entangled in a densely-vegetated stream bed. I heard a distant and muffled flare being fired. I looked up as a starburst split the sky with a trail of light. I watched it, then with a sudden fear and determination, forced myself over the log, tearing away the vines, battling to move forward.

I pulled out my map and compass. I traced the route with my finger to where it stopped, which should have been where I was. "This isn't here. This stream doesn't exist. Come on. Think! Ahead. It's got to be up ahead."

I put my equipment away, and forced my way through the undergrowth, untangling it as I went. Further on, exhausted, I squeezed through a few more inches.

I stopped, breathing hard. "I can't—I can't go—I just can't go—"

Taking a deep breath and holding it before letting it out, I heard a faint squelching sound close by. I let out my breath and tried to stifle my breathing. Then, I heard it.

Chapter Eleven

A radio squawked somewhere in the darkness ahead. I climbed up the side of the stream bed and, at the top, saw the beam of a red flashlight moving through the trees.

"I can't believe it."

I moved like lightning towards the light and the turn-in point where an instructor waited.

It was this little success—though more accident than anything I could really take credit for—that gave me the shot of adrenaline I needed to take one more step, then another, and another, toward the next point.

Moving on to my next point and much colder then, I ran down a dirt road. In the cold, steam rose from my nose, my mouth, my head, and my clothes. I weaved back and forth, stumbling. The dirt road thinned again, becoming uneven. I looked down at my wrist to check the time, forgetting my watch had been removed.

A soldier burst from the shadows, running toward me. As he passed, he snarled, "Point seventeen ain't out this way."

I continued to run, without acknowledging him. I started down a hill. The terrain was rocky, uneven, and deeply rutted. At the bottom, the trail narrowed again. I ran around a few corners, and up ahead, saw a candidate taking a reading from his compass, his faith bathed in its ghostly green luminescence.

I walked towards him. Up close, the candidate turned and looked at me.

"I'm out of here. We're lost." He moved past me and headed in the direction where I had just been.

I watched him for a moment, then looked back down the trail. I could not see more than a few feet in front of me. I pulled my compass out and took a reading. Then, I put my hands on my knees, bending over to take the load off my back.

"Come on, think. Think. Go back. Go back where? Everyone's going back. Come on, think."

Boom! A starburst rocketed through the trees back at the top of the hill where the last candidate was now. I watched it, noticing it light up the forest around me. I now saw the brightly lit trail in front of me. And something was there. The mud on the trail had been impressed with a fresh set of footprints. Getting down on my hands and knees, I felt for the boot prints and checked for any coming back. There were none.

"Hmmm." I took off down the trail. In the sky above, the starburst slowly fizzled out.

It was early morning, pre-dawn. I was exhausted, running and walking fast, counting, clicking down beads, taking readings with my compass as the sun began to rise. It had gotten even colder. My hair, runny nose, uniform – everything was frozen.

It began to snow. Down another dirt road, it was falling so thick I couldn't see where I was going, forcing me to slacken my pace. I pulled out my canteen, tilted it to my lips to find only a trickle coming out. I shook it, hearing the block of ice knocking inside. Putting it away, I stopped and looked surveying the trail ahead. A wide, waist-deep river blocked my path. Eerie, sharp, bone-like branches stuck out. This, according to the map, was Bones Fork River.

I pulled out my map again, seeing the routes I had covered so far. I had drawn lines, going from the left side, across to the right. I put the map away, looked down at my boots, then started to wade across, hoping for the best. The ice cold brown water came up to my waist. A wind came up and the snow fell heavier like a blizzard. Slowly and carefully I reached the other side and stopped.

After a moment, something caught my attention. In all

the stark white wilderness where nothing seemed clear anymore, the scent of smoke filled my senses. I followed the smell and saw a slight billowing of black-gray rising through the trees.

I crashed through bushes and branches. My compass was out, guiding me. I stopped, looked up, and saw a small fire and pick-up truck in the distance. I walked into the small camp. Four candidates sat under trees, frozen, exhausted, beaten, covering themselves with their green ponchos. They extended their boots out towards the small flame attempting to warm their feet. They all watched me as I passed by. I approached the driver's window. An evaluator sat inside with the heat on. I knocked on the glass.

Without looking, the Green Beret rolled down the window a quarter of an inch. I took the piece of paper I had been given at my last point and slid it through the window. My hands shook from the cold. The Green Beret looked at it, then at his watch and after a moment, said, "Okay, Seventy-six. Move out over there with the rest of them." The window went up.

I found a tree and collapsed on the ground. Snow fell, covering me like a pristine blanket.

A few hours later, Number Ninety-eight, a few other candidates and I were in the back of a canvas-covered truck rolling through the snow-covered countryside. Ninety-eight and I sat across from each other, closest to the front cab section. The vehicle started to pull away, then, suddenly, stopped.

An instructor from the front shouted back to us. "Make room for one more back there."

Hearing footsteps slowly crunching toward the back of the truck, we were shocked when Albert poked his head around the corner. He was frozen and shaking violently. He tried to speak, but his words were nothing more than mumbles.

One of the candidates muttered, "Wow."

Albert grabbed the top of the tailgate and tried to climb in. The candidates closest to him inside the truck pulled him aboard. He laid on the floor, still shaking, trying to speak. They started wrapping him up to get him warmer.

Albert finally managed to say, "Don . . . I—I knew—you'd make it." Albert looked over at me with a slight smile, as the truck began to pull away again. "No—no—heat stroke-today."

I looked at Albert for a moment, my heart breaking for his pain. My father's face flashed through my mind as a reminder, though; mind your own business and no one gets hurt.

After an awkward silence, I replied, "That's good, Al." Albert looked down at his feet and stammered, "I—I can't feel—any—thing."

I shook my head and moved toward him, got down on my hands and knees and reached my own frozen fingers toward Albert's laces. I knew what I would find. I glanced up and caught Albert's tear-filled eyes. I was rocked by the memory of my father's eyes. I just stared, unable to get a grip.

After a moment, another candidate spoke up and moved me out of the way.

"That's okay, buddy, we got ya. Let's get you on the seat and get those boots off."

I took my seat and watched the other men work on Albert's boots and steeled myself.

"Oh man! That's bad," says one of them.

I closed my eyes, knowing what they were seeing. A candidate yanked the other boot and sock off, gasping at Albert's frozen, swollen, and bloody feet. They went to work, putting his feet under their shirts, up against their bellies.

"We got to get his feet warmed up," one of the men

stated.

Another said, "Pull some gauze wrap out of my ruck for these blisters. They're infected bad."

I could feel Albert's hound dog gaze but I stayed focused looking at the floor and my own feet. I turned away as Albert whispered, "Don? Don? You alright, man?"

Team Week

It was a new day. The land navigation exercise was over and somehow both Albert and I survived. And back at the SFAS facility, a new phase of evaluation had begun.

Looking up at a loudspeaker on a pole, I heard the "Chordettes" 1954 recording,

"Mr. Sandman, bring me a dream, make him the cutest that I've ever seen..."*

Sitting on the ground while eating an MRE with Number Ninety-eight, I said, "What's that all about?"

The candidate casually looked up and told me, "Looks like team week's begun."

"What's that mean?" I asked, not sure I wanted to know too much.

"About a hundred and fifty miles of team endurance events."

I nodded and thought on that for a moment. "Why the song?"

"What? *Mr. Sandman*?" number Ninety-eight said with a grin. "Ol' Mr. Sandman. Why he's the first event."

With all I had already been through in SFAS, I was not sure I would be able to survive being on a team. Relying on others was not my strong suit. I could feel Ninety-eight's eyes on me, but I could not meet that gaze. I could not risk the observant candidate seeing the fear in my eyes.

We stood in the rain before the makings of a primitive structure which was about to force us to slacken our pace—four iron poles, crisscrossing at the center, like a tic-tac-toe board, from which sandbags were suspended sat. Albert, a few other candidates, and I picked up our ends and placed the poles behind our necks so it rode on our rucksacks. The obvious strain and pain could be seen in our faces. Albert and I led from the front left and right. Nearby, an evaluator took silent notes of our teamwork.

One of them asked the other, "How much does that thing weigh?"

"Not including those poles, their individual rucksacks, and equipment, I'd say about four-hundred pounds. Only ten miles, though."

The men laughed. Then the new man asked, "What's next?"

"Ammo crate carry. Another ten miles."

My team and I kept moving forward so focused on our heavy and torturous assignment that we forgot about the evaluators following: watching, taking notes.

It had been hours and we continued to walk. I, with head lowered and rain pouring off my face, struggled with each step. Each step felt like my last.

We were all exhausted. All of us had stumbled several times but no one spoke a word; we watched in unison as a Huey helicopter flew low overhead. A red and white medical cross was painted across its belly. It moved over the trees, out of sight.

My team walked up a steep, sandy hill with an evaluator following us. Every sinew burned in pain as we pulled our way over the top.

Albert shook his head and said, "Looks like someone else bit the dust. That isn't exactly encouraging."

One of the others tried to lighten the mood by answering, "You ever just wake up some mornings feeling like a pack mule?"

I did not even have the energy to talk, let alone joke. I

wanted to stay focused on the mission. "Come on. Let's get this thing done already."

From the top of the hill, I saw a road that went on forever. "Let's go. We're almost home," I said as I tried for some motivational encouragement.

The evaluators followed behind us, recording every actions, behavior, and conversation.

The sun was almost down and us exhausted candidates were walking by twos, struggling with yet another seemingly superhuman test.

Albert and I shuffled quickly and painfully with a long narrow ammo crate held between us. The cold, relentless rain had stopped.

Our skin had been rubbed clear off our wrists from the heavy load on the rope handles, and our fingers held the handle in a death grip.

Albert was barely hanging on. His handle started to slip, forcing his wrist to straighten. "I'm losing it! I'm losing it!" he cried to the team.

Angrily, I screamed, "Don't you drop it! Don't you do it!"

Albert in even greater distress yelled, "I can't hang on! It's slipping!"

I yelled back, "Come on! Don't you quit on me! Pick it up! We're running out of time!"

Albert admitted defeat, saying, "Let it down! Let it down!"

I screamed, No!" Then it dawned on me there was an alternative to failure in our grasp and I called out, "Switch!"

Everyone stopped, softly setting down the crates which were filled with simulated explosives.

Albert and I quickly switched sides, picked up the heavy crate and moved out again and regained speed and distance.

From a near distance, a Green Beret watched us slowly approach his location. By then we were carrying the crates with both hands, dragging ourselves along.

Albert and I made our way in silence.

Finally, the evaluator said, "Put 'em down."

Everyone dropped their crates and collapsed besides them.

Albert and I painfully lowered our crate, too.

Albert looked at his wrists, touching the deep wounds. I just looked at him and gave him a slight, albeit reluctant nod.

The long day and night of moving forward in extreme pain were over. For me, operating within the team framework had been almost as painful as the physical part of it. I could do the physical stuff and when it was over, it was over. I was raised to be tough. Much like my father's tirades, when they were over, they were over and I had survived them all, somehow.

But also, like those fear-filled childhood days, there were the unknowns. I preferred my lone wolf style. A weak link endangers both the team and the task.

Back at the SFAS facility, utterly exhausted, I grabbed my shower kit first thing and made my way to the latrine.

I was sitting on the toilet seat in a private stall. My back had been rubbed raw. I was staring down at my feet, almost too tired to move. Finally, I grabbed a bottle of NU-SKIN from my laundry bag. The front label read, *"NU-SKIN for minor blister irritation."*

So desperate for some relief from the pain that I never wanted to let people see, I also understood all too well the warning on the back label about not using it on open wounds.

I opened the bottle. After a moment, I looked down at my feet which looked far worse than a few days before. Swollen and discolored, infected blisters covered them. It was that stuff or gangrenes at that rate.

My kit included a small tub that I put my feet in. I leaned

over, hesitated, glanced around to check that I was still alone in the latrine, then stuffed a clean sock in my mouth to bite down on. I quickly poured the liquid over my feet.

The instantaneous and excruciating pain slammed me back into the toilet tank and I sucked in air through my nose. The sock muffled my screams and soaked up the tears running freely down my face. Convulsed with pain, I gripped the toilet paper dispenser and would have crushed it, had it not been metal.

Somehow, I kept my feet in the tub and after another long moment, the pain subsided and with tears still in my eyes, I stared at the back of the stall door, groaning deep in my throat. I pulled the sock out of my mouth and laid it over my knee.

I wondered if the cadre had noticed my behavior. Had I shown any sign of weakness? I almost chuckled. I probably had. How often had my father told me what a disappointment I was?

I was too tired to retrace my steps. Our time at Mackall was almost complete and I had done my best. Would it be good enough? I would find out on graduation day. Like so many other things in my life, I could not do any more to affect the outcome.

I pulled my feet out of the tub and gently patted them to be sure they were dry, then wrapped them as best I could with gauze and gently pulled on clean socks.

That time the first sergeant and his telltale cigarette were nowhere to be seen when I left the latrine. Back in the hospital-like ward, I busily repacked some equipment. The door opened, and a Green Beret entered, telling us to move out again for our final event.

The Final Ruck March

Some time had passed and the SFAS grounds were dark and quiet. Everything was calm except for the dark silhouettes which could be seen moving slowly to the other side of the small base.

Before long, all of the candidates were gathered at the starting position for the final event.

"Follow the green chem lights which are placed at one-hundred meter intervals. There is no set time limit. If you finish, you're doing well. Eight hours is not unheard of. Just do your best, gentlemen."

The first sergeant held up his stopwatch, clicked it and gave the command.

"Move out!"

Us remaining candidates started down the road to cover 28 miles as fast as humanly possible.

The first miles went quickly. At mile eight I ran through a small stream and others followed close behind. At mile fifteen, on a long stretch, green chem lights marked the way. I was in the lead, and there was another candidate twenty feet behind as we ran.

Around mile twenty-two, I was walking fast up a hill alone. I moved quietly up a section of old asphalt road and then over an old wooden bridge. I continued going and going, seemingly forever. I focused like always, but the adrenalin was gone. I would have been glad to have anyone's quiet company.

Another mile pounded beneath my throbbing feet. Now I was completely alone. The only sound was that of my boots hitting the ground and the swaying of my heavy ruck.

The chem lights seemed to go on forever. Finally, as I rounded a corner, I saw two medics standing outside a truck.

"What's your name?" they yelled in unison.

Sweating profusely, I answered, "Kabrich!"

"Where are you from?"

"San Jose!" I shouted.

I left the instructors watching me until I was out of sight

again.

A helicopter flew by, swooping low overhead. I watched it for a moment then continued to walk and run.

I was drenched with sweat, weaving back and forth like a drunken soldier. I stumbled, then started to run. Further along, I was too exhausted to even raise my head. Breathing hard I staggered down the road from one side to the other, my brain seemed to be sending mixed messages and my extremities responded in kind. Fluids dripped from my nose and mouth. Sweat pooled in my eyes. I was too tired to even try to wipe it away.

I looked up to see, like double vision, a mirage-like assortment of green chem lights dancing around. I was exhausted and my reserves were spent. The road lost shape and then came back. I hallucinated, seeing shadows running across the road, faces in the forest, green chem lights dripping eerie streams of fluorescent green fluid down trees into puddles on the road.

I heard voices laughing and screaming. Finally, I stumbled, collapsing into the dirt. I struggled mightily to get back up, wobbling. I looked back and did not see anyone else.

I lost track of all time and place, willing myself to keep moving forward.

On another seemingly endless stretch of dirt road, I shuffled, ran, and walked, almost unable to lift my feet. I went a few more steps. Then a few more. One more.

Finally, I dropped to my knees, too weak to do anything but stare blankly ahead.

"Rosssterrr Nummmberr Seventy-six."

In front of me was an evaluator. Looking down at his stopwatch and clip board he said matter-of-factly, "Time, Seventy-six: five hours, twenty minutes. Good job."

Selection Day

Around noon after everyone had finally made it back; we assembled in a classroom and were counted. We were eighty-five candidates standing exhausted but at attention.

The twenty-eight-mile road march ended a few hours before. Albert, number Ninety-eight, and myself were among those remaining. Moving to the front was the first sergeant followed by a few Green Berets. One of them handed him a piece of paper. There was silence as he unfolded and read it.

"Those of you standing in this room are among the few that can say they have completed this evaluation. You have all done a fine job and that's something to be proud of." He looked at us and allowed a full minute for his comments to sink into our benumbed brains.

"Evaluators! Move to the front now."

Five Green Berets moved to the front with the first sergeant. Number Ninety-eight was among that five. He passed by me, giving me a penetrating look.

The first sergeant continued. "These five men have been placed among your ranks at various times. They are all Green Berets sent to evaluate you from within."

I locked eyes with number Ninety-eight for a moment.

"If I call off your roster number, please, quietly leave the room. Those numbers are: 129—281—15—74—32—003—68—261—103—44—78—009—10—222—101—001—75—212—105—and—77."

Slowly candidates to the left and right turned and walked out. Albert and I were left in the ranks that remained in the room standing with several empty feet between us.

Sixty candidates remained when the last of those whose number were called left the room, closing the door behind them. Folding the piece of paper, the first sergeant tucked it into his pocket.

"Welcome to Special Forces school, gentlemen."

Number Ninety-eight smiled at me and the room broke into a quiet, tired celebration as we realized we were the group that had earned the right to continue.

The first sergeant quieted us. "Your training so far is just beginning, and over the next several months you will be tested in many ways. The hard truth is, out of the sixty of you in this room, maybe . . . maybe . . . a few of you will graduate with that class. And those who do will eventually be assigned to Special Forces A-teams. Just like the song says, *'One hundred men we'll test today, but only three win the Green Beret.'** Good luck, men."

I turned and started to head for the door. The first sergeant approached me.

"Kabrich, I expect to see you back here. You got a lot of training to do. Congratulations on drawing my crazy latrine talk. I do that the same time every cycle! It never gets old."

I looked at him in the eye and allowed a weary but heartfelt smile. "I'll be back." And then, looking down at my boots, I said, "Besides, I just got these boots broke in."

The first sergeant roared as though that was the funniest thing he had heard in forever.

I looked at him, then at the classroom of the few candidates remaining. I was done there and it was time to go to the next phase of training.

I walked out the door and saw some deuce and a half's waiting for us. On the pole, the loudspeaker started playing; *The Balled of the Green Beret.*

I stood and listened for a long moment, then picked up my gear, got on the truck and we drove away.

Chapter Twelve

Special Forces School

Week fifteen. I was deep in the North Carolina woods watching and waiting. The night was oil dark. All I could hear was the rain splashing down onto my green poncho shelter. The rhythmic sounds of steady dripping somehow provided a strange sense of peace and calm.

It was late and the once-swollen clouds finally retreated before a warm, nudging breeze from the east. I interpreted that as a signal that the storm had ceased; no more long, sizzling streaks of lighting or peels of angry thunder to shake pine cones and release showers of needles from the forest around me.

I peeked out from beneath the shelter of my well-worn poncho. Clouds raced to the north and beyond, and bright stars peeked now and then between the thick clouds.

Eventually, the moon broke through and illuminated the dense forest floor. As the large drops of water fell, puddles of trapped rain weighed down my shelter.

From somewhere amid a knot of pines, I heard the bulky, long whip antenna PRC 77 radio squelching, "Chuuuuuuuu.... Chuuuuuuuu." The faint glow of a fluorescent green chem light marked the tip of the radio's antenna. I surveyed the area, around which were several other mound-like shelters with steam rising from them, warmth escaping from the soldiers hunkered beneath.

This was a good reminder that I wasn't alone, that trainees like me were lying under their own ponchos. I put my head back inside my cocoon and soon drifted off to sleep.

At 12:30 a.m. I felt a tug on my poncho, it was my turn to take the security watch. I pulled the flap from over my head and the rain puddles washed my face, but I was so wet, what did it matter? At least the great deluge had stopped.

Now and then the radio squawked, reminded me of what I was about to do. At 1:00 a.m. exactly six of us would be handed our first set of coordinates. A ten hour, twenty-eight kilometer land navigation test was set to begin. It was an individual test. We would have to rely solely on our own wits and abilities to get through it.

I had done well with the far shorter SFAS distances but this one made me nervous. We had to find all four points on our coordinates within the short time allotted. Failure meant expulsion from the School. All that hard work would have been for nothing. I would either be "recycled" – made to start the entire Special Forces training over again by joining in with the next class – or dropped entirely from Special Forces training. The thought of repeating the entire fifteen weeks was too terrible to imagine.

This test, called the STAR exam – with a failure rate of fifty to sixty percent – was the most intimidating exercise. And bear in mind, that failure rate was among those who had summoned the grit and determination to stick it out through fourteen weeks of the most gut-busting, soul-crushing exercises you can imagine.

The terrain was unpredictable and varied from pine forests to thickly vegetated swampland like the infamous Bones Fork River. The moonlight did little more than turn everything into ghostly images, magnifying the sense of loneliness to which fatigue contributed greatly.

As I tucked my equipment away I could hear the other trainees doing the same. We weren't allowed to talk to each other. The green chem light hanging above the instructor's head provided a strange sense of comfort, much, I imagine, like a lighthouse to a sailor in unfamiliar seas. It was the only thing shining in that dark Carolina forest that night.

At 1:00 on the dot, the instructor, a sergeant, started calling us over. I had laid out my equipment before dark so I could find it, that way it wouldn't take me long to be ready.

My name was called.

I put on my seventy-pound rucksack and scrambled to his location. He gave me an eight-digit grid coordinate. I read it back to him and he wished me good luck.

I trotted away, bending to keep my head below the overhanging branches, and began to plot my course. My heart felt like it was beating out of my chest. This was it. Pass or fail. I checked and rechecked. The slightest miscalculation could send me hundreds of meters off target. The first leg was ten-kilometers.

We were warned that stumbling upon the waypoint at the end of that leg would be like finding the proverbial needle in a haystack. If we did, we'd find an instructor sitting next to a tree. The tree would have a four inch, red-painted ring, six-feet up the trunk. Since it would still be dark as pitch, I couldn't see how that knowledge would help much.

I shot my first magnetic azimuth of 148 degrees on my

compass. The filament, which provided my only light, contrasted sharply with the darkness around me. As I went in one direction, others passed me going in another.

I took off running, smashing through branches and jumping over bushes and logs. Though ten hours sounded like a long time, all four points could never be found by strolling along. I had learned that a long time ago.

Precise, pinpoint accuracy had to be accomplished at a high rate of speed. Any mistake would cost valuable minutes and, very likely, send me hopelessly off course.

I had to pick terrain features along the way as checkpoints – a ridge line, a road crossing, or the number of power lines overhead to confirm my route. The compass only served as a directional guide to get me to those places. When I got close, about 500 meters, I had to find my last unmistakable terrain feature corresponding to the map, called an "attack point." From there, I would be nose to the compass walking exactly the right number of steps in an exact direction, or miss my target and fail. If I needed to take my time to be precise, that was the place to do it.

Around 0500 I arrived at my attack point. I had traveled four hours through the dark and rain-soaked underbrush to get there, seeing no one along the way. The lights of a distant town or small city helped confirm my general direction because I had seen it on the map.

From the attack point, I walked in the direction the instructor point was supposed to be. The terrain became more dense and dark, and descended at a sharp decline.

The air had grown cooler and the sounds of brush more muffled. Like a blind man not even able to see my hand in front of my face, I carefully moved forward. I checked and rechecked my compass. My distance traveled, or pace count, had to be precise. Whatever was in front of me, I had to climb over, push through, or crawl under. I could not deviate from the precise compass reading. As I finished counting the paces to the instructor point, I stopped. There was nothing there. I just stood in a depression of thick brush in disbelief. Was I completely off course? Had I made a tragic error in my map plotting or utilization of check points? I didn't know.

All my senses were heightened. What I heard, smelled, and felt were all being analyzed instantly. At the same time, a sixth sense of sorts guided me. I fought off the panic. If I were an instructor, I thought, would I go into even deeper underbrush to set up a point? Not likely.

Conducting a 360-degree turn, I looked in every direction. After reviewing it in my mind, I was confident I was in the right place. Indecisiveness, doubt, or panic, had no place in Special Forces and certainly not while standing miles from civilization in a deep, dark place. My sixth sense allowed me to consider one last idea. Maybe the instructor point was obscured by trees or vines.

I got down on one knee where I could see from a different vantage point. I looked to my right, and where a moment ago there had been nothing, there was now the glow of a green chem light. I walked towards it, fixing my eyes on the green orb. It was so obscure I was afraid I would lose sight of it should it be obscured by a branch or tree. Within twenty meters I was standing at the foot of the instructor's tree, a one-man camp about six feet up among the branches where the light hung.

I felt like I had found the city of lights! The instructor just looked at me with indifference. "I could hear you out there and was wondering if you'd make it."

I handed him my slip of paper and sounded off with my name.

I only had six more hours to find three more points. With a new set of coordinates, I realized I had about the same distance to cover. I pointed my compass and moved into the dark and away from the sense of place and comfort that little green orb gave, leaving the indifferent instructor up his tree.

Running and jumping, clicking beads down on my pace count cord (counting every left step up to sixty-eight amounted to approximately one hundred meters traveled), checking and rechecking my compass readings, I attacked the thick forest eager to make up time. Sunrise gave me an added advantage of being able to see where I was going and to visually verify checkpoints.

Sweat mingled with the rain that I collected from every branch, bush and limb. I felt the weight of my rucksack on my shoulders and the fatigue starting to set in. I had less than three hours sleep in the last thirty-six.

As the sun rose, it brought with it heat and humidity. On my next point I was slightly off again and ate up valuable time searching for it. By the time I found it, I was down to my last three hours.

The atmosphere was leaden with heat. July in the North Carolina lowlands can be oppressively hot. To someone with seventy-five pounds of gear on his back running at top speed through fields and forests *oppressive* was an almost laughable understatement. For hours, exhausted almost beyond endurance, I'd been calling on every last ounce of my physical endurance and mental determination. I was afraid that if I stopped, even for an instant, I'd collapse.

So I ran. Soon my canteens were both empty. I was aware disaster loomed – that I was running the risk of heat stroke, possibly even heart attack – but I didn't care; I made a conscious decision to go all out. I'd gone too far to stop short of the goal.

By the time I reached the third coordinate I had only forty-five minutes left to find the last point. I still had several kilometers to cover, and there was no margin for error.

I decided not to take the time to fill my canteen. Across

open fields, up and over hills, and through pockets of forests, I moved as fast and as accurately as I could. I saw what I hoped was the last two-kilometer field. Everything in me screamed to stop before I boiled over.

I stopped sweating. That was bad. It meant I was severely dehydrated. But water could wait. It was all or nothing. If I died, I died. "Jesus," I said. It wasn't a curse, it was a prayer. Brief and to the point. I had reached the end of my resources, and I needed to borrow His. I took a deep breath and ran with all my might toward the finish line.

Fifteen-hundred meters later, my face bright red and my lungs burning, I stopped at the trees on the other side of the long field. It was the end of my pace count.

I didn't immediately see any sign of an instructor's location and I had no idea how much time I had left, but I most likely didn't have time to be off target. Right then I heard: "Report over here."

I was bent over, trying to catch my breath and, looking to my immediate right, saw my point location less than ten meters away. There were several other students already there sitting and resting against their packs. I stumbled forward, my piece of paper in my outstretched hand. The instructor – just as indifferent as the guy up the tree – took it.

"You cut it close. You have about ten minutes left."

I collapsed in the shade and my legs instantly cramped up. The other candidates just looked at me blankly as I guzzled down a fresh canteen of water. I had survived.

Not long after I had reported in, a truck came to pick us up. Getting back to the assembly area I saw hundreds of students sitting or milling about. I got off the truck and started moving towards the big crowd.

An instructor hollered, "Not that group. That's the test failures. Yours is the smaller one over there."

The smaller crowd had about forty students. We had

lost seventy-five percent of the class. I was one of the few to pass the land navigation test. As I observed the groups more closely, I noticed the failed group included soldiers wearing splints, head dressings, eye patches with Iv's sprouting from their arms.

The training had been the most grueling I'd ever known. Fact is, had I known how tough it would be beforehand, I'd probably have let my Rambo dreams just die. In the end, the majority of students failed, some were sent back to start with a new class, a few survived.

In earning the right to wear the Green Beret I'd been admitted to an exclusive club, but one from which - I was left in no doubt - I would be promptly and unceremoniously expelled if, at any time, my performance, actions, or behavior brought dishonor to the unit.

Chapter Thirteen

Special Forces teams are comprised of four Sgt.-level specialists: Weapons Sergeant, Engineer Sergeant, Communications Sergeant, and Medical Specialist. Teams are designed so that no matter where in the world they might be dropped off they could be self-sufficient in conducting training and operations. I became an Engineer Sergeant. In addition to learning all phases of construction, I was also taught demolitions; in other words, to build and destroy.

After training in all other types of engineering, I was given extensive and intense training to become an expert with explosives. For several weeks I spent time in a classroom or on an explosives range. In the classroom, after learning bridge design, I learned bridge destruction; how to precisely calculate the proper type, amount, and placement of explosives a particular job required. Doing that required an in-depth understanding of how bridges and other structures were built. This knowledge helped me judge how much of a delay time to set, and determine the destructive capacity required to effectively sabotage the structure to the exact degree the mission required.

Each day I was tasked with working out exact mathematical equations and formulas that supported a given scenario or mission. I had to figure out if I needed a slow explosion or fast, several delays in detonation or none, where to most accurately place the charges to best facilitate the effect, and whether or not the charges would require tamping (burying).

Destroying a bridge with multiple spans together with its abutments, required hours of detailed planning and laborious computations. In the end, the exact amount of explosives to be carried in for the mission and the exact timing for detonation using time fuse calculations had to be correct.

Also covered in demolitions training were mine and booby traps or "improvised explosives devices (IEDs)." We had to memorize all types of anti-personnel and vehicle mines. The pace was fast and mistakes equaled dismissal, as did failure to meet other course standards.

Of the original thirty-plus students only eight of us were cleared to move on to the third and final phase. We were placed on a team together to conduct simulated team operations. After several days of planning in isolation we set out on one such mission.

Hide-Site Mission

Standing in the dark on the lowered tailgate of a C-130, I saw the hills and trees race by out of sight below me. There were 230 extra pounds of rucksack dangling at my knees and parachute equipment hanging off my back. Camouflage paint crisscrossed my face. I held onto my parachute chord to help steady me. The plane bumped severely in the turbulence caused by the hot, humid air, banking back and forth as it flew low over the North Carolina countryside.

Not too low, I hoped.

We stood one behind another and a single red bulb dimly lit the interior. The sound of the wind and engines was too loud to yell over. My eyes burned from the plane's exhaust. White, steam-like air slithered out one vent and into others. My back stitched with pain under the load as I straightened up in readiness. I couldn't wait to jump, to feel the tug of the jet stream, and relief from that burden.

This was phase three of Special Forces school and my mock twelve-man operational detachment (Alpha) - ODA - was conducting a reconnaissance training mission. The task was to parachute undetected behind enemy lines and set up a "hide site," or hidden reconnaissance base from which to survey a major enemy supply route.

For a week our team had researched, planned, and rehearsed the mission. Every aspect of the training mission was treated as real. Being the engineer I had to come up with a hide site construction plan. Materials in exact amounts had to be parachuted in. In addition, each man carried at least nine quarts, or two gallons plus, of water. Everything had to be jumped in with us; food, water, ammunition, hide site materials, and other pieces of tactical equipment.

Suddenly the jump light turned from red to green.

The first man ran, jumping off the lowered tailgate into a sea of black and then I could see a faint silhouette of his parachute ripping open. The remaining pack tray of the parachute and its chord whipped in the jet stream, slamming against the sides of the ramp opening. One by one we ran, lunging off the ramp. I followed the line taking me to the tailgate and forcefully stepped into the void.

For a moment I was violently slapped around in a maelstrom of air currents and lost my stomach from dropping so quickly. I counted to myself, almost willing my chute to rip open. A few seconds later I felt the gliding, lifting effect of a full canopy over my head. Total silence and peace rushed into my senses as I watched the outline of the plane fade out of my vision. All around me I could faintly see the other chutes floating down across the sky.

I steered through the darkness and into the wind I could soon make out faint details in the countryside below, including the open field that was our drop zone. The distinction between it and the surrounding vegetation was only slight, but became more evident as the ground rushed up at me.

Reaching down, I pulled the release strap and watched my rucksack fall to the end of its line, twenty feet below me, swaying side to side. Pulling my steering toggle I made one last turn, making sure I was facing into the wind. The ground came up quickly. At first it was just a view from above but it turned into a very personal reality. Treetops, limbs, and bushes were all flashing by me in startling detail.

The knee-high grass took shape and the descent speed seemed too fast. I braced for the landing putting my feet together and elbows in. My whole body was trying to anticipate impact. I heard my rucksack slam into the ground, and gritted my teeth. Hitting the ground concussed the air from my lungs. I grunted with the pain of a controlled crash landing. My feet stung, and my hip absorbed the full weight of my body hitting the ground as I continued to roll onto my shoulders and back. The crashing finally ended and I lay still.

The parachute fluttered quietly as it settled into the grass next to me. It seemed to say, "This is how it's done." Sounds of the countryside began to claim my senses, as did the smell of the wet grass and the fresh earth beneath it. The last of the parachutes floated down and disappeared beneath in the tall grass. The airborne operation was over .

My body was soaked in sweat making my uniform stick to my skin. I gathered my parachute and stuffed it away, then collected my rucksack and pulled it over my shoulders. It seemed, somehow, to have gained weight during the descent. The team members assembled nearby in a wooded area. No words were spoken. Only an oft-practiced gesture or quick arm signal was necessary. Everyone understood the mission and their role in it. It was still too dark to see clearly, as we slowly filed through the underbrush and disappeared into the forest.

We walked all night, often stopping to conduct silent map checks and crossing danger areas in order to remain undetected. At times, we only moved a few hundred meters. Slow, silent, and methodical, we pressed ahead. With each passing hour, my pack dug deeper into my muscles until the straps felt like they were resting on shoulder and collar bones. My knees ached from kneeling whenever we halted for security checks.

On a slight, almost invisible trail, a whisper was passed back down the line. It was one word: "Hole." A huge depression had to be avoided. Like the kids game 'Operator' I passed the word back to the man behind me. It turned out he thought I said "hold," so he stayed put while the rest of the file marched on. However, as he was losing sight of us, he decided to catch up, and face the consequence.

He fell into the hole.

The full 180 pounds carefully balanced between his shoulder blades suddenly shifted and propelled him downward. Stumbling, he managed to catch himself after several half steps. I'm sure extreme pain traveled down his shoulders and spine to his hips and knees. Finally, he recovered, and crawled back in step behind me. There was no crying or whimpering or anger. No emotion. It was something to be ignored; a non-issue. The mission was in front of him.

As the sun began to rise we descended into our patrol base – a thick layer of vines, brush, and low hanging tree branches. We blended easily into our surroundings. Once again, in response to a quick hand signal we spread out, forming a circular perimeter. Kneeling and lying behind a fallen log or other concealing piece of vegetation, we scanned our sectors, prepared to respond to an attack from any direction. It was so quiet we could hear if a twig snapped 150 feet away. Finally, another signal passed around the perimeter, and we began our next stage.

An operations center was set up in the center of the circle and security elements were pushed out to serve as a listening and observation team. Once assured of our relative safety and security, we were able to relax our security posture in order to prepare for the next phase of the operation.

According to the map, we were just a few kilometers from the chosen hide-site location. We made as little motion as possible. Only radio checks were conducted or drinks of water taken. Equipment for the night movement was quietly prepositioned for ease of identification. The hours drifted by slow and heavy beneath the scorching North Carolina sun. The air was suffocating. The thickets seemed to creak in protest as the sun dried them to kindling. Twelve hours had passed, and besides a few recon missions, we just waited. Finally, day gave way to night and we could once again own the darkness.

It was time. I had cross-loaded* everything the team would need to set up and occupy the hide sight. In a very short time, in order to assure secrecy of the mission, every team member had a separate role to play. Each man carried what was specific to his role for quickly getting the job done. The team had to trust me. I had researched and practiced the exact formula for constructing the hide sight.

Since we were to leave no trace of having been there, some creativity and thinking outside the box was required on my part. At first the team didn't grasp the purpose of my unconventional approach, which was this:

Besides carrying enough food, water, and recon equipment to last several days inside a concealed hole in the ground, I made the team carry metal electrical conduit poles, chicken wire, tarps and sandbags. Most confusing to them was the requirement I gave them to carry black trash bags full of pine needles. The pine needles were collected just outside the patrol base. When it was safe enough to move, we advanced slowly and carefully to the site's location.

Small advance teams were sent ahead to observe any signs of enemy forces. The training scenario had us infiltrating deep behind enemy lines. Being detected or having our security compromised was not an option.

Upon arriving, we spotted the major supply road where we needed to set up and monitor. 150 meters behind the road were mounds that naturally covered the pine-forested hillside. I decided to build the hide site above the road and among the mounds. Graders and observers would soon come behind us, trying to find signs of our progress that would lead them to the hide. My job was to make sure they had nothing to follow, and couldn't find us even if they came within a few feet of our position.

Our team filed on to the location I had chosen through my study of aerial photos. Fortunately, the plan was simple – limited time and low visibility left us no other option. We took off our rucksacks and some of us laid out the equipment. The rest of us started quietly digging.

The area I had measured and staked out was nine by nine feet square. We had to dig deep so we could hide below ground level, and we had to dig in the dark. Ever-conscious of not leaving any trace of our existence, I had the diggers – of whom I was one – put every shovel full of dirt in one of the sand bags we'd brought with us. These, when full, were packed tightly around the edges of the hole. In all, we dug three feet deep and stacked the sandbags another three feet, for six feet of protection.

Once that was complete, the telescoping metal poles were extended and used to form a framework over one end of the square. To make them sturdy, I laid them out in a grid, bent them into shape and taped each intersection. I had the team overlay this grid with the chicken wire and, over that we made a roof of the thick plastic tarps. Lastly, the men emptied the pine straw from their garbage bags over the entire structure spreading and blending it in with the rest of the natural ground cover.

Within an hour or so the hide site was complete and

looked like just another natural mound among many on the hillside. Within it, two or three men could remain hidden in relative comfort for days. Two hollowed-out coffee cans were shoved through the front of the hide site and camouflaged; through these we could observe any activity in the vicinity.

For some of us, this would be our home for the next few days, when they'd be replaced by another set of observers. With the first team inserted, the rest of us sealed them in, closing the back of the hide, and crawled back the way we'd come. As we retreated we carefully brushed all the disturbed ground back into place, covering every trace of our passing.

Back at the edge of the thicket, we took one last look. In the foreground all we saw were the silhouettes of hills dotted with identical looking pine straw mounds. We had successfully and stealthily designed, constructed, and inserted an invisible team to conduct surveillance. The hard part was next: living in the hole and lying still for two to three days.

Green Beret Won

Showing what we could do as a team and doing it successfully was one of many final exams given in Special Forces school. Proving that we were good teammates, excellent at our jobs, and an invaluable asset to missions, won us our Green Berets. So many had set out to achieve that goal. In the end so few had actually made it.

In the back of my mind I still thought I had gotten away with something. In other words, I don't think I believed I really should have been chosen. Not even in that very impressive personal moment could I really think myself good enough. But I couldn't dwell on that for long. Whatever I thought, the Army had determined me worthy, and I held the proof in my hand, my Green Beret.

I graduated in the top ten percent of my class. I'd done it! I had finally proven my dad wrong on all accounts; I *was* smart, I *was* tough, I *was* strong, and I *did* amount to something. The truth was that, in becoming deadly - to be feared - I was satisfying my flesh and my pride. I was still a Christian, of course, so I justified that pride by wrapping it up in a philosophical mix of jingoism and patriotism.

Mission accomplished.

It was time to move on to my permanent assignment and a Special Forces team.

Chapter Fourteen

Fort Campbell and 5th Special Forces Group (SFG), where I was first assigned, is located in Clarksville, Tennessee about 45 minutes northwest of Nashville. Fort Campbell was also home to the 101st Infantry. Both units were legendary. The 101st was a battle-tested infantry unit with a history going back to WWII, and its exploits were chronicled in HBO's *Band Of Brothers* series.

The 5th SFG was highly successful in Vietnam where they collected numerous unit citations and numerous Congressional Medals of Honor. John Wayne financed, produced, and starred in a movie about the unit called *The Green Berets* back in the late 1960s, and it's considered a classic.

Several years after the Vietnam War, 5th Group moved, making its home a few streets down from the 101st at Fort Campbell. The Special Forces Command has created other SFGs each with responsibility in a specific world region. 5th Group covers the Middle East, Southwest Asia and some of East Africa. Those regions were evolving as the most volatile and strategically important in the post-Vietnam era. 5th Group would take on this important assignment.

The Group was located in buildings similar to those in our compound in Germany: three stories, tan, cinder block constructions built sometime in the 1960s. On the first floor were team rooms, offices, arms rooms, and storage areas. The rooms on the second and third floors were occupied by six twelve-man units per floor.

In the space between the buildings, small obstacle and strength-training paraphernalia – chin-up bars, suspended logs, climbing ropes, etc. – were set about. The buildings themselves were arrayed in a quadrangle around a large grass parade field. By the time I arrived in late 1995, the place looked shopworn and neglected. Inside, old metal desks, painted battleship gray – and just about as heavy – were backed by file cabinets painted a kind of government - issue bile green.

Wear-and-tear aside, the scene could have been lifted from any U.S. Army base, circa 1945.

I reported into the company sergeant major whose office was at the end of the hall directly across from the commander's office. There the motif was, if anything, even more outdated and severe, the only concession to comfort being a vinyl couch with cracked and sagging cushions. The faded, 60's-era linoleum was dull and deeply scuffed by thousands of boots. Over time, they'd worn a little bare patch clear through to the concrete about three feet in front of the desk where the Sergeant Major sat, writing.

I positioned myself in the middle of this little island, and waited. Eventually, without preamble, he stood up and pointed at the dry erase board on the wall. Various colors were used to denote dates, names, numbers, and box-lettered matrices. "Where am I going to put you?" he said, talking more to himself than me. Nevertheless I pointed to the scuba team. "I'd like to try that," I said.

He looked me up and down with some surprise. "You would, would you?"

"Yes, Sergeant Major." Fateful words, those. Looking back now, I can appreciate his surprise. To him it was as if I'd said, "I'd like to go to the Abyss, Sergeant Major."

He wasted no time arranging the paperwork and telling me where to report. With just a twinge of apprehension, I stood before the Scuba Team door – which was festooned with an assortment of decals portraying Great White sharks in attack mode and other dive-related subjects – raised my hand, and knocked. The door flew open and I stepped into a strange new dimension.

Up until that time, most of the soldiers I'd encountered in Special Forces, though intense, were soft-spoken and very much by the book. In contrast, the atmosphere in that room sizzled with in-your-face aggression. It was immediately clear that this was a fraternity, and I wasn't about to step into it without proving myself.

Several team members in various stages of uniform were sitting or standing around a large table in the middle of the room. I was suddenly peppered with questions about my swimming ability, my current level of physical fitness, my training, etc. I answered these as best I could in the few seconds I was allowed to respond. Finally one of them interrupted me. "As for your mental state, we already know you're an idiot."

It was absurd, of course, but the question flashed across my mind: "Has he been talking to my dad?"

"You'd have to be to volunteer for this duty."

I decided not to point out the irony that this made them all idiots, too. The questions continued, and each of my answers drew guffaws and shakes of the head. No answer was the right answer, and all my experience counted for nothing. I was making a first impression the exact opposite of what I'd intended.

After the introductions and jokes subsided, I became more or less invisible. They spoke about me as if I wasn't there, talking about the trouble I was going to cause them, how they'd have to delay missions to save my life or at least forestall my death for a time.

In my naivete I had signed up for what very few others in SF ever earned: the coveted "SCUBA Bubble" badge.

Over the next six months I learned that my previous Special Forces training had been the equivalent of nursery school.

Scuba Training

The indoor swimming pool on post was an eerie place. Like everything else, it was old and decrepit. It was also dark, and humid; the water deep and the pool long. Once I was in the water, I demonstrated my basic swimming skills. I was told to swim underwater from one end of the pool to the other and back again. That would have been half the length of a football field. I thought they were just harassing me. There was no way that was a real requirement.

They also wanted me to strap on twin 80 dive tanks, a buoyancy compensator floatation (BCF) collar, an eighteen-pound weight belt, a mask, and fins. My job was to move away from the side of the pool into the deep end, put my hands in the air, and keep my head above water somehow for five minutes. "Right," I said, "And then I'll leap a tall building in a single bound." Of course what they were asking was humanly impossible.

Suddenly they stopped laughing. They weren't kidding. But they weren't done yet. They also told me to tie three ropes into separate knots – two very short ropes with the last knot being almost impossible to complete – while on the bottom of the pool. That would take a couple of minutes, kneeling on the bottom while I wrestled with the stiff ropes.

Another exercise required me to take all my dive gear off a few pieces at a time and lay them on the bottom of the pool in a perfect predetermined arrangement. Then I had to dive down and put on all the gear. Lastly, I put on my dive mask, cleared all the water out of it, and slowly fin to the surface, blowing all the air out of my lungs as I ascended.

These tests were designed to push me to the absolute end of endurance, each one lasting a minute or more beyond the point I thought I couldn't hold my breath a second more. The purpose was to get me used to the feeling of drowning, that was the only way I could keep from panicking in real-life situations. Panic would lead to death. Even worse, it could endanger the team and the mission.

To say I was humbled that first day in the pool would be an understatement. The team had left me no doubt what I'd signed up for. I was lying on the pool deck, soaking wet, in shock, humiliated, and feeling like my head was going to explode. "That's good," said one of the team guys. "You lay there and take a little nap. It's going to get worse. A lot worse."

It was January in Tennessee and the team prepared me the best they could for the next few weeks. I ran until I puked, did push-ups, sit ups, and rope climbs until I could do no more and, of course, I spent several hours a day in the pool. The idea of swimming the length of half a football field on a single breath seemed a less superhuman task every day. By the end, I was dragging a weight belt while scratching the bottom of the pool to get to the other end and back, ever increasing my breath-holding capacity.

Within a few weeks of continuous training I was faster, stronger, and more capable of accomplishing the once laughable water tasks. In time I began to feel perfectly at home in the water.

One exercise, called drown-proofing, involved having my hands tied behind my back and my feet bound together and being thrown in the water for twenty minutes. My only instruction? "Survive." Even that task became run-of-the-mill in the final days.

The team began looking for pre-scuba classes being held elsewhere and, despite the progress I'd made, I secretly prayed they wouldn't find one. I didn't feel ready. I needed a lot more time. To my horror, the team sergeant came into class one morning, beaming from ear-to-ear, bursting with the "good news" that they'd found a pre-scuba class at Fort Bragg, North Carolina. In February.

A short, stocky, pit bull of a team sergeant and his team of sadists were in charge of the pre-scuba training. Special Forces guys came from all over the country to be there. The course was run under strict guidelines and, though its official mission was to prepare candidates for scuba school, in practice their job was to do everything they could to break you and make you fail. There was no grading on the curve, either you won through, or your went home.

For me, failure was not an option. By the time the final day of the course had arrived I'd spent hundreds of hours in the pool, run sub-six-minute miles all over Fort Bragg, conducted thousands of pushups, flutter kicks, and pull-ups, and climbed several hundred feet of rope. I needed a medic to give me a shot to numb my right hip flexor to dampen the sharp pain caused by the over-exertion from finning*.

I wasn't sure exactly when it happened, but I suddenly realized most of the other students were gone. After a blur of two weeks and eighteen-hour days I stood in formation – one of only three to survive the course – to receive the coveted "Recommendation to Attend the Combat Diver Course."

The ceremony took place on an otherwise abandoned parade field, under a cold, low, late-winter sky. Elsewhere in the world there were college athletes who'd receive multi-million dollar contracts and national adulation because they could run a hundred yards in ten seconds and throw a ball.

For us – three guys who'd just come through weeks of unremitting mental and emotional root-canals – this was it. No adulation. No millions. Our prize?

Survived.

A crisp "Well done," followed by a handshake and a hasty "Good-bye," and I was off to scuba school in Florida. Despite all I'd been through, all the mental and physical hurdles I'd cleared, as the countryside rolled by on that ten hour drive, I had to keep repeating to myself "You can do this. You can do this."

At the same time another voice, from somewhere deep inside was shouting, "You can't do this. You're going to fail."

Soon I was in Key West, Florida, at Trumbo Point Annex

and, before I knew it, halfway through Dive School.

By this time, I was consuming over ten thousand calories a day and still as skinny as a rail. We all were, burning through all those calories, and then some, in each twenty-four hour training interval. Typically, after shoveling down the evening meal, it was time to conduct a night navigation dive, where speed and accuracy were critical.

In the darkness the dive boats bobbed in the ocean. Their engines idled, forming a thin layer of smog on the surface of the water. Two by two, like ghostly silhouettes, dive buddy teams sat on the side of the boat, facing inward, ready to flip over the side.

Each of us wore a Draeger rebreather system with two black hoses running from the mouthpiece. We were holding lines, buoys, and compass boards, all of which were plenty to get tangled up in. Our masks were slightly fogged up as we breathed through the astronaut-like apparatai. The instructor barked, "Enter the water!" and backwards we went over the side. The boat backed down as we disappeared near the bow of the boat. I got one last compass reading, gave a thumbs-down signal, and prepared to disappear below.

The beach was hard to see so far away. A pre-stationed vehicle with its headlights on was all I had to guide me – at this distance, they were nothing but a pin-prick in the darkness. We descended to eighteen feet, just above the sand and grass bottom. The only light was the illumination coming from the green glow-stick attached to my compass board, on which was also a watch and depth gauge.

We were wholly dependent on those gauges as we swam. It was not unlike flying an aircraft solely by instrumentation. Side-by-side, we were aware of one-another's presence by the slight compression of the water as we finned quickly and silently in the direction of the compass heading.

As I swam, I continually checked my gauges and oxygen levels. My breathing was fast and heavy, like running at

pace for several miles. The rebreather kept cycling the same air over and over, filtering it through the chemical granules to make it breathable again. A high-pitched sound could be heard on occasion informing me that now the Draeger was mixing a bit of new oxygen with the stale recycled breath. It was always like breathing half a breath though. The lungs wanted so much more, but the small rebreather bag only provided so much volume. Nevertheless, I continued to fin.

The beach didn't seem to be getting any closer. My legs burned with pain as I continued, pushing the water and propelling my fins through it. The sweat and heat were almost unbearable. Waves of anxiety assaulted me. "Is this compass broken?" "Have I stayed on heading?" "Is there enough breathable air left in the system?" "Am I going to pass out?" "Is the rig failing and poisoning me?" "Can I keep going at this pace?" "Are we close?"

I felt like a kid whining in the backseat of the car: "Are we there yet?"

Hours went by in darkness. The silence was only broken by my own rhythmic breathing. My ears started to respond to change in pressure, and the water temperature changed slightly. The debris passing my hands and face changed too. Slowly the depth gauge rose in feet. Another hour passed. We slowed down so as to not disturb the surface. Soon the water was knee-deep.

We ascended together, half expecting to have drifted miles off course since we entered the water. Amazingly, we were only fifty meters off course. The truck and headlights were to my immediate right. The onshore instructor saw us and yelled, "What's your dive team number?"

We shouted it out.

Exhausted and cramped, I slipped off my fins and tried to stand straight or bend my ankles, but they had been in another position for so long as I adjusted to life ashore – a world dominated by light, and sound, and gravity. It was like being reborn. I ran down the beach to the assembly area, glad to be able to breathe fresh air again.

Scuba Graduation But Still Not Worthy

There was something about being a Green Beret that satisfied me on a very deep level. I felt best when conditions were the worst. Simply put, I liked suffering. It felt good. I was accomplishing several things by always struggling against my limits. In a way, I suppose I was continuing the abuse that I felt I deserved. It was the right way to treat someone who was inadequate, a disappointment to his father. I saw my military challenges, in fact all my life, as punishment for sins – whether real, imagined, or simply imputed. All my training was a kind of self-flagellation, like those Christian penitents who – feeling unworthy of Jesus' sacrifice or, even worse, that Christ's sacrifice was not sufficient to atone for their sins – walk miles barefoot over stony ground until their feet are a bloody pulp, and whip themselves until their flesh hangs in shreds from their bodies.

I could relate.

Comfort and ease made me uncomfortable and uneasy – and guilty. Abuse was my normal. Being shown love and respect was not, and always felt foreign to me. Perversely, I felt suffering was a way of getting back at my father. I wanted him to repent for having abused and abandoning me. That was ridiculous, of course. He had no clue of the torment I was putting myself through – and couldn't have cared less if he did.

Then again, he'd take credit for my military successes, if he knew of them: praise himself, during his drunken stupor, for having raised a Green Beret. I could never let that happen.

Chapter Fifteen

As I write, I'm reminded of my worst night as a kid. I was startled awake in the dead of night. I sat erect in the darkness of my room, wide-eyed with terror. From downstairs, I could hear yelling, screaming, and things crashing. In my pajamas, too scared to sit still, I threw off my covers and, with my heart in my throat, raced to the hallway as my sister, just two years old, emerged from her room.

In order to honor my sister's wish that her part in my life's story be kept private, I will leave her trials and travails to your imagination.

This is the one exception, as she proved so brave this night. We froze and our eyes frantically searched darkness at the foot of the stairs. We flinched at the sound of another crash. The violence was worse than unusual. My sister, standing beside me in her nightgown, suddenly started to wail and ran down the stairs. I followed.

Rounding the banister at the bottom of the stairs we ran through the kitchen and the living room towards the screams. In a small white bathroom, the terror was unveiled.

Our dad was kneeling on Mom's arms. She was flat on her back, in a long white sleeping gown, he was pummeling her with blow after blow. Each blow got more ferocious. She kicked and screamed in terror. My sister screamed and jumped on his back while I stood in the doorway frozen in fear.

Dad left off beating Mom and tried to stand with my sister on his back. Like a drunken bear, he stumbled and staggered, but my sister's arms were still clutched tightly around his neck. My mother struggled to her feet and tried to get past him. He lunged for her as she ran by. The small bathroom echoed her cries of pain. My sister released her hold, dropped from our Father's back to her feet and ran to Mom. I was still frozen in the doorway.

As my dad stood, panting with blood smeared across his shirt, his eyes met mine; they were the eyes of a demon. His fierce gaze looked right through me. That man was not my father. It must have been someone else; a soulless monster possessed by rage. He came after me and I ran, dodging his outstretched arms. He stumbled and fell into a planter sending it crashing to the floor beneath him. Dirt, pottery and green leaves stuck to his hands as he slowly rose.

When he spoke, he spat venomous threats about wanting to kill us all. They came like the growl of a cornered animal. My mother, sister, and I huddled in a corner as he bounced off bookcases and door jams and finally stumbled past us toward the stairs, which he crawled up on all fours. I got to my feet, trembling. My mother pushed the two of us quickly through the house toward the front door. Rounding the corner at the top of the stairs, my father returned. He snapped a magazine into his Colt 45 handgun. Mom screamed, tore open the front door and, at three in the morning, pushed us down the driveway and into the street.

The bullets we expected to come did not and in the black silence of the night, in a neighborhood like any other, we ran down the quiet streets. No words were said and the only sounds heard were our bare feet slapping the cool asphalt. Around the corner we hid in a large bush and crouched in the dirt like hunted animals. We listened intently. In the distance, a few dogs barked. An occasional cricket squeaked. Nothing had to be said. Before long, our heads were nestled in our mother's lap. I stared up at her beautiful but bruised and bloodied face. The glow from the rising sun began to lighten the dark sky and she started humming, gently rocking back and forth.

I closed my tired eyes and her tears rained on my face.

It was the memory of that night, and others like it, that defined me, that formed the foundation, the root of emotional chaos and tumult that sent shoots through every fiber of my being. I was a five and ten years old with PTSD, and I'd spent a life trying to outrun it, or at least to silence it.

By the time I completed Scuba School, PTSD had been part of me for so long, it was normal. I needed it. It was an adrenaline pump, pushing, and shoving, and kicking me through all nine circles of satanic oppression. I realize now that it was all a vicious circle of needing abuse and hating it at the same time. I couldn't live with it, and life was worthless without it. I was a junky, and my drug was self-contempt.

As a result of this irreconcilable need for both punishment and vindication, I sought the most difficult and stressful trainings the service had to offer: Jumpmaster, air assault, advanced demolitions, weapons training, and anything else I could find, all in order to live inside my PTSD comfort zone.

The rush was what fueled me, and the 5th Special Forces Group offered it up in heaping helpings. We tortured ourselves with painful PT in the mornings, and stimulated our adrenaline needs with airborne jumps in the afternoon. We also had the typical army sessions of vehicle maintenance, team equipment inventories, and standing in what seemed like thousands of formations.

Regardless, everything revolved around the deployments, specifically deployments to train and work with other countries' military special operations units. I spent approximately eight months a year away from home conducting deployments to places like Pakistan – deep into the country near the Cashmere region; into Kenya and on the Somali border; in the mountains of Yemen near the Red Sea; in Oman, conducting airborne jumps into the Arabian

Sea; and in small boat operations and desert operations in places like Qatar and Kuwait.

It seemed that I was always somewhere other than home. Finally, the day came when we went off to war. For all the reasons mentioned earlier, it was where I felt I ultimately belonged, where I would receive the ultimate punishment, or absolution; the place I could prove I was worthy, and take up permanent residence in my comfort zone: trauma.

The phone might ring, or a knock sound at the door – without warning – at any time, day or night. Within hours I could be anywhere in world. It was a feeling I never quite got used to, being in my living room one moment and the next in a dusty, foreign place where everyone seemed to want me dead.

5th Group had it all: sacrifice, suffering, punishment, adrenaline, fear and fury. Hell had become my heaven.

Through it all, though, God's still, small voice was whispering to me, in foxholes, deep in the ocean, hanging from a parachute over enemy territory in the dead of night saying, "Whenever you're ready."

That's all.

That was too easy. Only in places of peril and deprivation did I think I could experience anything really meaningful or peaceful. Only constant striving to overcome every obstacle, every challenge – on my own – would make me worthy. Only then could I be a son. Only then could I be a father.

Going to Iraq

You have to be a little crazy – or suicidal – to volunteer to go to a war zone to join a combat team on the front lines. It's called "going advance party." If that sounds like we're going to the park to make sure all the party reservations are in order, well, not so much.

Going Advance Party meant being deployed a few weeks before and alone with limited resources and security into the front-line area of operations to link-up with the ODA you will be replacing at the battle front.

On this first of three times I volunteered to do this I was over Mosul, Iraq. Finally there, my C-130 aircraft started diving, spiraling straight down to the landing strip. We were advised to lock and load our weapons and I knew it had just gotten real. It was dark outside and the pilots were launching star clusters* off the aft end of the aircraft.

Early on, a soldier's children learn the meaning of "Good-bye."

This was done in an attempt to misdirect any heat-seeking missile attacks.

We sat in the cargo netting under the glow of a red tactical light. My helmet was on and gear ready to go. The huge aircraft spun faster and faster down, and then suddenly did some sort of controlled hard landing like on an aircraft carrier. For a moment, it was hard to tell if we'd crashed or landed. It turned out to be the latter.

Pretty quickly the tailgate dropped down and it was pitch black out. Noise and light discipline were being enforced. It reminded me of what it must have been like to land in Vietnam. Stepping into the night, we wandered aim-

In a place with no cover, you're always a target

lessly, looking lost while the seasoned veterans herded us together and shuttled us off the tarmac as quickly as possible. In the distance, I could hear the unmistakable drone of helicopters and automatic gun fire.

We boarded a transport vehicle and were immediately bombarded by Madonna's *Holiday*. The irony was typical of life in the combat zone.

We threw our gear in a nearby tent and racked out. The next morning we were ordered to the command tent, where the team we were coming to relieve would pick us up. "So," I thought, "we're just gonna drive through the enemy city to get there in broad daylight?"

The answer was, "Yes."

War in Iraq was learning to roll with the punches. I went from being home and never feeling danger and being able to predict that I would be alive for the foreseeable future, to knowing I could get killed at any moment, right then and there. Sure enough, it wasn't long before the other team in their machine gun mounted Humvees came rolling in. We had a short briefing and then off we went.

In broad daylight.

The skyline all around the city was rung like construction was taking place, as if the whole city was being rebuilt. I could see stuff going on in every direction. Fighter jets screamed by, helicopters fired mini-guns at a hillsides, explosions resounded in the distance, and an endless parade of trucks and other military vehicles streamed by, all to the soundtrack of Madonna singing *Holiday*.

Could it get any more surreal?

The first thing we did once we left the relative safety of the base was run directly into a massive traffic jam. Everyone looked like a combatant to me. Our very seasoned team inched through, sirens blaring, and occasionally throwing rocks at cars to get them to move. There was a lot of cursing and finally we broke free of the deadly dance.

I was relieved when we got through the traffic and sped across the city via the expressway. Before I knew it we were winding our way up a hill to our patrol base and what, I hoped and expected, would be some semblance of security.

Not the case.

It wasn't long before I realized that the base was on top of our hill, meaning we stood out as an excellent target. All I could think was "some politician picked this site!"

Mortar rounds whistled in. I watched everyone else for what to do. I saw my panic reflected on their faces. Everyone dove for cover. In time the bombardment stopped and the dust settled. One-by-one we crawled out into the open.

"Welcome to Iraq," said someone. "You must be special. They don't greet just anyone this way. See if you can stay alive."

For a few minutes after that, I got special treatment as the incoming new team member sent to relieve them. I learned we were on an old missile base. I was given a brief tour which ended up on the far side of the base, in the middle of which was a bubbling cauldron of green goo. Knowing Saddam's proclivity for poison concoctions, I could have done without that. It was some sort of biohazard for sure. I wondered if it glowed in the dark.

The eventful day gave way to a tense night. The poor privates out on the perimeter were getting spooked, convinced the enemy had breached the wire surrounding the base. We had to mount a patrol and go hunting for them in the tall grass and abandoned buildings. It was the first time I ever really thought about getting shot. Where would the bullet hit? I took inventory. A leg or an arm, I could survive – or a foot, or a hand. Shoulder? Probably. Torso, that would depend on whether my bullet-proof vest performed as advertised. A head shot? This would be good-bye. For some weird reason, though, I felt like any bullet with my name on it would hit me directly in the face.

Okay, top of the list: don't get shot in the face.

Check.

Fortunately it was a false alarm, but it drove home the fact that I was no longer in training; this was war. Real war.

Even in war, though, there are places of relative safety. Even comfort.

This was not one of them.

The next morning, surveying the situation, I realized that my appraisal of the previous evening had been optimistic. I'd landed smack in the middle of a killing zone and death was all around me. As I looked out over the city from our high ground, I was reminded of a Bible study I'd attended once. That night it had been about Jonah and the whale; a story about faith, disobedience, and consequences. In the story, Jonah had been sent to warn the city of Nineveh that God was going to destroy it if its citizens didn't repent and change their ways.

Much to Jonah's surprise, they did.

Today, that city is called Mosul – and that's the city I was looking at. Even though I stood there on top of that hill feeling like a great sniper's target, I Like Jonah, prayed over the city that day.

Chapter Sixteen

Wars are like books; they need a title: the *Korean Conflict, World War II, the War of the Roses*. I guess that's to differentiate them from one another in the long, sad history of mankind's alarmingly successful effort to overturn the Golden Rule. Someone had called this war *Operation Iraqi Freedom* and it had officially begun several months before. When, a few weeks later, the rest of my team arrived at the base, they received orders to get ready to mount a convoy: imminent departure.

At that moment, I was on the firing range assisting with training. Even though I was busy, I felt like something was wrong. I had a sense of foreboding. I started asking questions of the men around me. "Where is everyone?"

It turned out we were tasked with taking the team we were replacing back to a nearby Forward Operating Base (FOB) called Diamondback on the other side of the city.

My heart suddenly jumped; I needed to be with my team. I scampered up the dirt bank to find several vehicles waiting. I was overwhelmed by a sense of urgency – responsibility – to help protect those men. After all, having arrived a few weeks earlier, I knew the area better than anyone. Everyone was deep in preparation as I approached the convoy, adrenaline pumping through my veins. This was it, all I'd been training for. The realization was both exciting and terrifying. Engines were revved, radios squawked, and orders seemed to be flying all over the place.

To the untrained eye, it was chaos, but I saw the order in it. Everything was being done to purpose. Then I grasped a horrifying reality and excitement gave way to horror; the only place left for me was shotgun – right front seat – of a light-skinned Humvee; the only one without armor protection.

We got the "Go!" command. Despite my misgivings, I

strapped myself into the unprotected seat. I was shocked the vehicle was even part of the convoy; it stuck out like a sore thumb. Unlike the other vehicles in the convoy, it had no armored turret, no bulletproof glass, no three-inch-thick armor reinforcement. This thing couldn't survive a run-in with a Yugo, and I knew it. But it was too late to do anything about it.

Had I gotten there a minute or two earlier, I could have advised against using that vehicle. As it was, the convoy was already rolling out the gate; my teammates were already strapped in. I choked down my apprehension, jumped in that deathtrap and slammed the flimsy door behind me.

The driver's name was Mike. Pete, my junior, was standing in the turret hole. Then Andy, another long-time member of the team, showed up at the last instant and jumped in back. The atmosphere was tense and I know everyone was thinking what I was thinking; this is not good.

But we were soldiers; we accepted our orders, carried them out, and kept our concerns to ourselves. If anything, we attempted to promote confidence to help the situation. Somebody above us in the chain of command must know what they're doing.

I just hoped it wasn't the same guy who decided to station our post at the top of a hill.

"I love you guys," I yelled over the loud engine and fan motor to try and break the tension that lined every face. Everyone just kept their thoughts to themselves, their senses acute, heightened by danger.

We were all maxed-out with gear – helmets, eye protection, armor-plated vests – and held our weapons in a ready position to react to any immediate threats.

The lead vehicle pulled out of the gate. Sandwiched between it and the following vehicles was my team in our soccer-mom Humvee. I steeled myself, settling into my seat and occupied myself by checking systems, adjusting my equipment, and keeping my eye on our location on my hand-held GPS unit.

Soon the convoy had snaked outside the wire – a definite point of demarcation, feeling like the point of no return.

I took one last look at our pathetic situation. Internally I felt devastated. Windows were down, the sheet metal doors rattled, and Pete – armed with only an M-4 assault rifle – stood in the hole where there should have been an armored turret and machine gun. He was completely exposed.

Andy, sitting in the back on a bench seat, was also exposed. Over the din, I yelled at Pete to come down, but he couldn't hear me. I yelled louder. Still there was no reaction. Either Pete didn't hear me or he was just too focused to notice.

The convoy snaked down the hill, taking a right onto a deserted boulevard. Soon we were in the middle of a typical Iraqi urban neighborhood; abandoned stores, mud huts, and rusting fences lined the streets. Billboards in Arabic lined the street and shop fronts huddled in little islands of color amidst the otherwise dry, dusty debris-strewn city.

The convoy made a U-turn crawling up and over a three-foot-high median.

We were finally on our way to the on-ramp. Once on the highway we could travel at top speed to Diamondback.

We'd left the first phase of danger behind. To our right, a fifteen-foot-high plaster wall hugged the road in a gentle curve. I used my arm to keep from falling towards the driver's side as we kept veering sharply right. I had a sudden premonition about what a whole panel of glass might feel like if it suddenly exploded in my face.

I rolled down the window, glanced at the wall, then to the front again. Just as my eyes drew the sight through the windshield into focus, a huge explosion slammed me to my right.

Surreal had just become more surreal.

I felt like I was submerged, swimming and spinning as if caught in a giant wave. I don't recall any sight in particular; no sound. Only darkness. Despite the floating sensation, I was completely aware of where I was and what had happened. Somehow I knew the sensation of being submerged would end and I would burst back into the moment.

Strange as it seems, I distinctly recall feeling oddly peaceful in that moment. This was it. The end. Then I was back, staring at the blackened deformed windshield. The Humvee was bumping and weaving in a cloud of smoke, debris and heat. I looked at Mike who was too busy driving to spare me a return glance. He was trying to get us to safety after what had been a bomb blast to the right side of our vehicle. My ears rang with a high-pitched whine, and things seemed to be unfolding in slow-motion. Somewhere, as if from another world, or muffled by a pillow, I heard Pete scream out in pain. Someone yelled into the radio. "We're hit! We're hit!"

Parts of my body started to burn and ache and my entire right arm was numb. What if I looked and it wasn't even there anymore? For a moment, I almost smiled at the irony. We'd been blown up. *I* had been blown up!

Mike had managed to wrangle our smoldering Humvee to a stop about a hundred meters from the point of impact. I seized a moment to take a mental inventory of my body from top to bottom. Arms and hands? Check. Legs and feet? Check. Whether they were working or not remained to be seen.

Pulse? Check.

The other vehicles disgorged the troops and they were swarming by in controlled panic. Someone shouted at Mike to get out and run to a nearby position to pull security*.

Our guys carefully extracted Pete from the turret. It was

obvious he was in great pain. Within seconds, I found myself alone. I took my helmet off and dropped it and – with the dazed fragments that remained of my senses surveyed the situation. We had pulled off the on-ramp and onto an adjacent road. Everyone was responding to the command to secure the area, but they all seemed to be going in different directions.

The right side of my vehicle was severely damaged. Most likely, two 81mm mortars had been taped together and packed with nails and bolts for extra shrapnel effect. I estimated the epicenter of the blast – judging from the condition of the vehicle – to have been twelve to fifteen feet away.

Our Humvee a few days after the attack.

I felt like someone had hit me in the side of the face

with a baseball bat and I could smell my burnt hair and eyebrows. It was hard to see out the windows, make out what was happening, or know where we were exactly. I tried to reach the door handle to get out, but couldn't. I felt as if I was half-paralyzed with a double force of gravity pushing down on me. Suddenly, I was more exhausted than I'd ever been.

I ran my hand over my chest, legs, and down to my feet. Apprehensively, I checked my face. I was relieved it felt like it was okay. Blood was dripping, but I couldn't tell from where. Finally, I looked at my right arm; it was there. However, an entire section of uniform had been ripped away at the elbow and blood was pumping out like an upended oil can. An entire chunk of my right elbow had been blown away by the blast. Two inches of my brachial artery were gone.

Even before we came to a stop, I'd already lost the critical pressure and blood volume to function. I was going to bleed out. I tried to reach my wounded arm with my other but for some reason, it wasn't possible. I wanted to cut off the blood flow. I looked around and tried to call for help, but my voice was too weak to carry. I realized I would probably die right there within a matter of minutes.

I raised my arm up onto the windowsill to elevate and slow the flow of blood. I could hear the team working on Pete and it sounded like things were as bad as they could get. In fact, Pete had been hit in his ear just under the helmet by a large piece of shrapnel that penetrated deep. I leaned back, hoping I could relax my breathing and pulse to slow the loss of blood. Just then, a teammate ran by asking me if I was okay. I wanted to say, "Yes. And . . ." but all I could manage to get out was, "Yes."

And just like that my help was gone.

I couldn't put together a meaningful sentence. I tried to pray but found that was also impossible. All my thoughts just seemed to end.

Suddenly, my heart skipped a beat and it labored to find a new rhythm. My breathing was shallow and difficult. I was doing everything I could to stay awake, but it was no use. "Oh no. Not yet," I thought. I realized that dying wasn't painful or scary, just unexpected. And there was no pain or sadness because my mind was drifting away slowly. It was just tiring. Just before my eyes closed, I watched the smoky, cracked and deformed Humvee windshield fade to black.

It seemed like many hours had passed, but it was probably only minutes when I opened my eyes to see who was calling my name. I swiveled my head slightly to see the team medic bent over at the door's window. He said a few comforting words and I nodded in agreement. Like a man trying to survive a journey through the desert with no water, I was mentally exhausted.

The medic ran his hands around my head, behind my back, then my legs quickly checking for more serious wounds. Breathing heavily and sweating profusely, he pulled a nylon tourniquet out of his kit and turned it tight, then tighter around my right arm. I knew it was necessary, but the pain was unbearable; then he twisted two more times.

Like a water faucet shut off, the bright red flow stopped.

I tried to speak but couldn't say more than two words of any significance. The medic told me he would be back and, with that, was gone. Once again I was alone with my fragmented thoughts.

I struggled with the fact that we had been hit. I wondered who hit us? From where? Who else was wounded? Had anyone been killed? As my thoughts continued, the pain on the right side of my face began to escalate. Simultaneously, I marveled at the complete lack of feeling in my right hand and arm. My gaze drifted to the floor; a pool of blood filled the entire floor pan.

My blood.

I saw the jagged holes where shrapnel had torn through the door and walls of the vehicle. I thought the whole right front side of the vehicle must have been shredded and torn.

The medic returned with a few more teammates to recover me from the Humvee. They pulled me up, then out of the seat. I draped my good arm around the shoulder of one of them and, together, they half-carried me to another Humvee. Just like that, I escaped my coffin and isolation and was headed into the light.

They placed me hurriedly into the back seat but I noticed their looks of concern. I tried to lighten the mood for them – they didn't need to be worried about me. I thought of that corny old movie line, "Tell my wife* and kids I love them." Unfortunately, I was unable to apply the necessary humorous twist to it. With every additional word I attempted, I realized I couldn't make my brain function.

Pete and I were transported to a small, nearby medical facility. Though only ten-minutes away, it seemed to take an eternity to get there. An old Marine-style Quonset hut sat on the corner of a small military outpost nestled in the middle of a walled and secured section of some former Iraqi government-type base. I was pulled from the back seat and carried towards the tent sporting a large red cross on a square white background. The tents were semi-structures in that they had doors and windows and some sectional walls and flooring. A medic in scrubs waited at the door already wearing surgical gloves.

The swinging doors were slammed aside by the gurney as they wheeled me to the operating theater, and my senses were bombarded by intense, tightly-orchestrated chaos. Orderlies, nurses, medics, and doctors moved in orderly array with a practiced purpose. A team of medical personnel grabbed me, pushing, prodding, poking, and peppering me with rapid-fire questions.

"Blood type?"

"Where have you been hit?"

"What happened?"

"Can you feel that?"

Holding my right arm, the doctor touched different spots on my hand and arm. I couldn't feel anything. He asked me to move my fingers. With all my might, I couldn't make the slightest movement. I was lifted onto a table. They cut my boots, trousers and shirt off, and then piled my body armor and helmet on top of it all and stacked it in the corner.

Five people at once were sticking IVs in my arm, inserting catheters, and flashing lights in my eyes and ears. My right side felt heavy, like a thousand pounds of pain and discomfort. Even with all that, I couldn't help but be impressed by the efficiency and professionalism of the medical team – and what they were doing in that tent in the middle of nowhere.

A few feet away, when I was able to think outside myself, I heard Pete moan in pain. Looking over, I could see his arms and legs in constant motion, as if they were trying, independently, to escape the hurt-shaped hole at the core of his being.

My doctor announced my condition to his team. "Right temporal lobe penetration, left hypothalamus, lower cranial, soft tissue, tympanic, nasal cavity pressure and metal frag, fluids unremarkable, burn, right side face and hair, open right shoulder, graze, brachial separation and tissue, paralysis, left leg undetermined penetration, left top foot chemical or fragment, third degree," etc.

Though nothing I could say would be of any help, I wanted nothing more than to know how Pete was doing? What had happened to the rest of the team? Where were they? But I'd lost the ability to communicate.

The medical team cleaned and re-wrapped my wounds adding fresh bandages to my neck, the side of the head, and my left leg and foot. I just lay there under the clear rubber oxygen mask. I scanned the operating room and saw heaps of bloody gloves and gauze laying everywhere. My ears still rang loudly and ambient sounds were muffled and distant.

In the strange world into which I'd been thrust with such violence, life was so profoundly different than it had been just twenty minutes before. I was no longer an armor-wearing warrior, but a soot-faced, bloody casualty. My armor was a thread-thin blue hospital gown. My enemies, hordes of unseen germs and bacteria.

I couldn't hear much or speak at all. I couldn't even keep a thought straight. I had most likely suffered a stroke. I just lay there staring at my pile of combat equipment and listening to the cries of my helpless buddy.

The doctors administered a sedative and the medevac helicopter swooped onto the pad just before dark. I watched the compartment door slide open and – amid the thunderous concussions of the blades and the clouds of debris they kicked up I felt suddenly vulnerable. Maybe the worst thought of all was that I couldn't defend myself, let alone anyone else. Now I was just a piece of damaged Army equipment that needed to be quickly transported back to Forward Operating Base Diamondback.

A medic leaned over to shield me from the prop-wash until we got to the loading point. Four soldiers ran my stretcher out to the awaiting helo and slid me into one of the four stretcher rows. I felt like my nose was scraping the bottom of whatever was just above me. Claustrophobia set in. I couldn't see or hear anything, just the helicopter blades. I laid in my slot vibrating and rocking in the belly of the great mechanical beast as it idled. Time dragged by and I waited for something, anything, to happen. Finally, with darkness all around me, I could see figures at my feet loading someone above me. It was Pete. Once we were secured in our slots, the helicopter rapidly powered up and rose in a cloud of dust, immediately banking sharply to clear enemy fire.

Even as a kid enduring my father's violent, drunken tirades chasing me through the house, I hadn't felt so vulnerable, weak and scared as I felt laying flat on my back in the pitch black helicopter. I had envisioned the helo ride differently; more like me and Pete lying on the deck where a medic kept us company. But no, this was like an airborne bus operation that made more stops, picking up more wounded as it leapfrogged its way to FO3 Diamondback.

Chapter Seventeen

I awoke to my company commander, team sergeant and a unit chief warrant officer huddled over me like biologists inspecting a specimen. I couldn't make sense of where I was or why. All I knew was it was time to get up. I said, "Let's go." Then I whispered, "I need to find . . ." But I   couldn't get my body to do what I wanted it to do.

"Just hang in there and lie back down, soldier," my CO told me with a pat on my shoulder. Recognizing my disorientation, the warrant officer, a former medic, got down eye to eye with me. "You guys got hit. You're at Diamondback. We got you." With that, I went unconscious.

It seemed only a moment later when I woke up again. I'd been flown by Medivac to Camp Speicher in Tikrit, an hour away. This time, an entire surgical team wearing masks was encircling me. "What is your blood type?" the surgeon asked.

I answered in a barely audible whisper "Where am I?"

The Army doctor seemed annoyed. He said, "You're in the combat support hospital in Tikrit. Just relax." I thought, Saddam's hometown? this can't be good.

I was sedated. As my eyes closed, I heard the nurse running me mechanically through what they were going to be doing.

I felt the metal bars pry open my mouth and slip over my tongue. She told me to relax and not swallow. I figured they were trying to open my throat and insert a breathing tube. The nurse continued her instructions. I tried to relax, telling myself this was all part of the procedure, but something was wrong. She fed the tube down alongside the cold steel of the laryngoscope*.

I tried to accommodate her by opening my throat as wide as I could. Then it happened. The tube made it extremely difficult to breathe around and panic set in. I fought to get air around the tube that was blocking my efforts.

The nurse sounded angry. "Relax. Don't breathe around it. Let it breathe for you." I didn't understand. Let what breathe for me? What was she talking about? She told the surgeon, "He's breathing around it," as though she didn't know I was awake. That's when I understood – I wasn't supposed to be!

The surgeon replied, "Pump the ball all the way up." I knew exactly what that meant. And it meant that what little air I was getting would be completely blocked off.

Pumping the ball, the nurse kept up her mantra: "Stop fighting it. Let the machine breathe for you." I felt the hose expand completely and the promised air didn't fill my lungs. Total panic set in and I started convulsing. I tried to get away from her, to pull the tube out, but my wrists were strapped and the team was holding me down.

"Put him under!" voices screamed in unison. I flailed, frantically trying to get air. "He's awake. Put him under!" the doctor ordered someone. My body heaved and my legs kicked as I waited for the madness to end. My body was responding to the panic and lack of oxygen, but my mind was counting on the team to get me under quickly. The last thing I thought was how much all of the thrashing must be further injuring my right arm.

After the surgery it was another helo ride. This time, I woke up in a hospital recovery room and air was rhythmically and steadily being pushed into my lungs through a tube. I felt the air go in perfectly and thought, "Oh. So, that's what it feels like." Fully awake, I managed to swallow around the tube. I wanted it out. I wanted it out immediately. I felt stupid having a machine breathe for me when I could do that myself.

When the orderly and nurses came in my room, I motioned for them to remove the tube. Slowly they inched the tube out until at last, I was free of it. Looking myself over in the light of day, I was covered in bruises. As I was able, in a raspy voice I asked, "Where am I?"

"Baghdad," was the reply. "The two of you will be going to Rhein-Main near Frankfurt, Germany shortly."

I looked across the room and saw Pete propped up in his bed. I immediately noticed his breathing tube and how he was scratching and pulling at it. Something wasn't right about how Pete was acting. He was awake and aware one minute, then he drifted into states of varying consciousness the next. For the most part, the medical team attributed his behavior to fatigue and shock. No one knew the small hole in his right ear was as serious as it turned out to be, or that he could have suffered brain damage.

I knew that Pete had been wounded just eight months earlier in Al Ramadi, Iraq while they were clearing a house of insurgents. His body was bound to be susceptible to infection. He'd been shot in the calf muscle of his left leg, but it was a through and through wound, meaning the bullet had entered and exited without hitting any bone.

My friend, Master Sergeant Kevin Morehead,* (who was Pete's team sergeant) and a medic on another team had been killed. I wondered if that injury had anything to do with what Pete was experiencing now. While I contemplated this, Pete was transported to Germany leaving me to worry about him. While I hated being separated from him, I was as incapable of helping him as I was to help myself.

When it was my turn to move on to Germany, I was wheeled to the front doors of the hospital and waited with a few familiar faces to see me off. Among them was my old sergeant major.

When I had left Key West and my Dive Instructor position, I was re-assigned to 5th Special Forces Group. Upon my return there in October 2003, I was initially assigned for a short time to 2nd Battalion, Bravo Company to a Mountain team - which specialized in mountain climbing! I was not thrilled about this at the time. The war was on! Sergeant Major was my company sergeant major and coincidentally also lived in my neighborhood. We ran together on some of our days off. I showed him a few running routes I liked. I wanted to get back on my dive team in 3rd Battalion, so I was only in his company for 7 months. Ironically, when I got wounded, he was stationed for a combat tour in Baghdad on the base near the hospital to which I was transferred for a few days. I was very weak and could not talk much, but his face was one of the faces I recognized and I took great comfort in his presence. I can't recall the company commander's name, but he, too, dropped in from time-to-time and that was encouraging.

In Baghdad, Sergeant Major P. had been assigned as military liaison in Baghdad, along with my company commander. They made small talk with me for a few minutes, never mentioning the burned hair or my charred face. When it was time, they escorted my gurney out to the helicopter, helped load me aboard and waved a farewell as the chopper lifted off. I was flown to the nearby air base and loaded onto a plane headed for Germany. It was just another leg of a long, long journey.

Descending from the clouds, my transport landed at Rhein-Main Air Base where it was rainy, cool, and green. I was taken by ambulance to another hospital. This time, Pete and I were in adjacent rooms. Though I couldn't see him, I felt a certain heaviness for him, one I couldn't explain. An older, distinguished-looking surgeon came into my room and told me a delicate procedure would be required to remove a large nail head from the back of my skull. The shrapnel had stopped just millimeters from my spinal cord at my brain stem and was crimping off the flow of the cerebral artery that supplied blood to my brain and blood vessels. If the object was left in place and then jolted or moved in any way, it could sever the artery. For the fourth or fifth time in two weeks, I was put under general anesthesia and woke in unfamiliar surroundings, affixed to an assortment of tubes, wires, and a breathing machine.

While in recovery, a visiting doctor noticed my dirty and unshaven face. He approached the bed and smiled, "We can't let you go home looking like this, now can we?" He cleaned and shaved my face. Soon after that, fresh gauze bandages were applied to my new four-inch incision at the back of my head. As I was wheeled out my surgeon came alongside the gurney and handed me a small sealed plastic cup. "Thought you might like to have the thing that almost got you," he said. I took the cup and looked inside; a quarter-inch-diameter nail head rattled against the sides as I shook the cup. I released a long sigh as I stared at it, slowly shaking my head. That tiny piece of metal had altered the course of my life.

Finally, en route to the States and Dover Air Base in Washington D.C., it seemed like I had the medical C-5 airplane all to myself. Although there were many two and three-bed high stretchers throughout, I was the only patient. All the other passengers were returning medical personnel rotating out and back to the US. On a bottom row, somewhere in the middle of the maze of stretchers, I laid with an I.V. hanging above my head. Except for my assigned nurse, few others paid any attention to me. Their minds were on home. They were excited and energized having survived another deployment; finally about to leave the war behind, and get back to their loved ones. There was laughing and joking, loud talking and fun chatter all around me; but I was in another place, in a different frame of mind. I felt small and insignificant – out of place. I asked for a sedative or pain medicine so I could escape the loneliness for a while. I closed my eyes and listened to the low roar of the wind and engines, wondering how Pete was doing. He was on my mind when, at last, the medication and engine drone lulled me to sleep.

Dover Air Base, Washington, D.C.
At two in the morning there wasn't much activity at the end of the taxiway. It was dark with no sound but that of jet engines powering down. The tail ramp had been lowered and I lay on my stretcher listening to the others talk among themselves as they deplaned and boarded a shuttle bus. My attendant and I were left alone in the middle of the runway. I didn't know what we were waiting for and, after a couple of minutes, was just about to ask when a vehicle drove up. A soldier got out and approached me. He draped a patriotic blanket across my chest and then saluted. "On behalf of a grateful nation, thank you for your honor and sacrifice."

In the middle of the night, in the dark, on a deserted tarmac, I listened to the words the soldier had probably recited a hundred times before. Then he helped load me into the ambulance and drove away.

Unconsciously I projected the image of my father on that retreating figure, leaving me all but alone somewhere ignored and insignificant.

I was transported to Walter Reed hospital and admitted to the Intensive Care Unit. As they wheeled me through the doors, I was struck by the fact that less than five days had passed since the explosion.

At the hospital, my wounds were reevaluated, cleaned and redressed and I began the long process of rehabilitation and recovery. My wife, Karen,* and my mother visited, staying nearby. A few guys from 5th Group also showed up. I was set up with future surgical procedures, follow-up appointments and a myriad of medical things to accomplish.

After two weeks I was able to visit Pete. He was one

floor above me in a long-term ward. His parents had passed on, but Karen and I were glad to meet his wife and sisters and immediately did everything we could to help them. It gave me some focus – a reason to get up each morning. The worry and frustration on their faces touched me deeply.

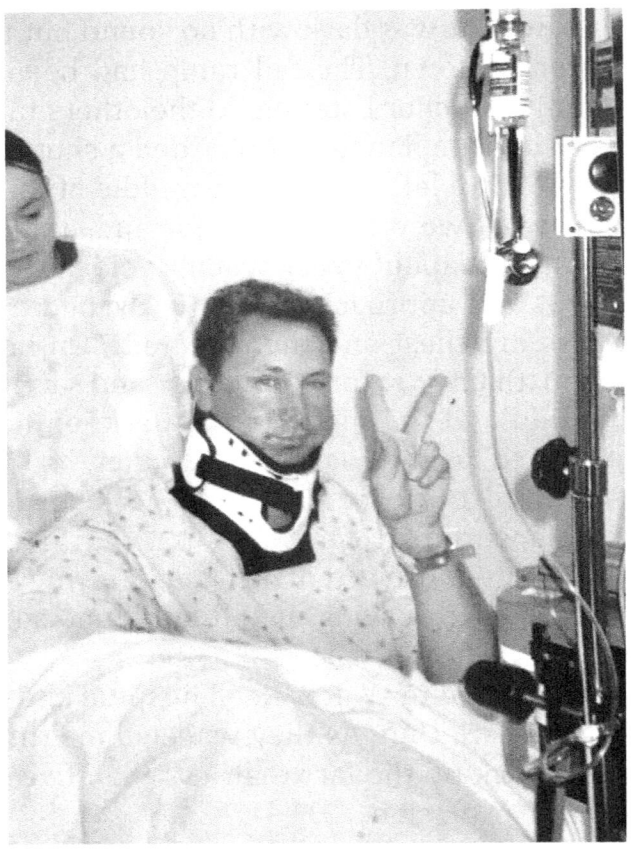

Pete wasn't getting any better, and no one knew why. He looked bad. I tried to be an advocate of sorts, stepping in to get better care for him or, at least, some answers. The injury to his head made it hard for him to communicate clearly and because he still had a tube coming out of his windpipe, he couldn't verbalize anything. When he wanted to communicate, he had to write it down.

Sometimes it was hard for any of them to understand what he needed or how he truly felt. To make matters worse, the doctors weren't providing much information or any real prognosis. The busy ward was understaffed and getting any quality personal medical attention was almost impossible. We rarely saw the same doctor twice; most of them were doing some form of residency. The bottom line was: Pete wasn't getting better.

Though my energy was limited, I tried to help. If nothing else, I hoped I was an encouraging friend to Pete and his family. I longed to make sure that he knew how valuable and appreciated he was. Several days later it was time for me to be discharged and sent back to my home base hospital at Fort Campbell for continuing care. After sharing a smile and handshake with Pete, we gave everyone in the family a hug and said goodbye. As I walked down the hall for the last time, tears welled in my eyes because I felt like I was abandoning my friend at the worst possible time. But there was nothing else I could do.

Once again Pete and I were separated. I hoped we would be able to reconnect again once he arrived back at the hospital in Fort Campbell. Regardless, I knew I had to get better, too. I could not change the things that had happened. It was time to leave. I needed to survive Walter Reed.

At Fort Campbell they prepared me for recovery with bed rest and medications. There were x-rays, rehabilitation, constant tests and follow-up appointments to keep. Most of my unit was still deployed, so I was on my own to get through whatever recovery I could.

I worried about Pete and often called his wife and sisters for updates only to find that things were not getting better. I had my own problems, as it seemed I was getting lost in the medical system too. Every doctor or provider had to be told repeatedly why I was there, what my injuries were, what had happened, and what was currently ailing me. I was on ten or more different medications including antibiotics, nerve pills, stool softeners, and various pain relievers. I had to sleep on my back with my arm and leg elevated, careful to keep the right side of my head from touching the pillow. Every wound oozed and throbbed and swelled.

I woke up in cold sweats. My legs ran every night as though I was fleeing from something. I woke up gasping for breath like I was suffocating. Because of the trauma to the right side of my head, specifically to my eardrum and inner ear, the room spun all the time. Whenever I moved, it spun more and more until I became nauseous and would throw up into a bucket beside my bed.

Lying there for hours on end, I stared at my heavily bandaged right arm. I endured waves of burning and aching pain. My right hand and fingers were totally paralyzed. I wondered if I would ever be able to use my damaged arm again.

At long last, a doctor performed a nerve conduction test on my arm. He applied electric leads to different muscles from my fingers all the way up to the top of my arm. A microphone made crackling sounds when the doctor touched each spot with a probe. He shook his head repeatedly as he listened to the intensified crackling sound.

The test revealed that my nerves had been severely damaged or severed entirely. The doctor politely told me that my hand had very little chance of improving. I carried my dead arm home completely demoralized.

I had been home almost three months when my team sergeant in Iraq called and asked me to come back to help them out. Ten thousand miles away, he had no idea what my condition was and no one had thought to keep him posted. I explained that the doctors wouldn't release me yet.

Thirty days later I got the word that another incident occurred in Iraq and another one from my unit had become a casualty. The major – commander of Company D – had been killed by a mortar attack. They returned his body to the States to be buried in Arlington National Cemetery. I requested permission to attend the service and the request was granted. I also saw the trip as an opportunity to see Pete at nearby Walter Reed.

Chapter Eighteen

I still needed help getting dressed. With only one working hand, I couldn't button my shirt or lace and tie my boots. I had just enough energy to make the trip and attend the funeral. After the service, I made my way to Walter Reed and found Pete still in his hospital bed. His wife was by his side and it didn't look like much had changed. What was obvious to me was that Pete looked gaunt, gray, and totally lethargic. I was instantly confused because the doctors talked as though he was getting better, but he looked far worse. He was scheduled for a routine surgery to stimulate a damaged nerve in his face.

As I sat at his bedside, I realized how much we had bonded since the IED incident.

We were intimately connected by our shared experience. I knew I was the only one in the room that could truly know what he was feeling. I held back my tears careful not to ruin the optimism he had reserved for the day. His family may have thought he was on the road to recovery, but it was clear to me that he wasn't.

Because the doctors needed to prep him for the surgery my visit was brief, but I promised to stop by the next day. We shared a look and a handshake and said goodbye one more time. I hugged Pete's wife and told her not to worry, and then made my way back to the hotel.

At two in the morning I was awakened by a knock on the door, which I opened to find one of the soldiers in charge of my trip standing there. "Pete died," he said, matter-of-factly. "He didn't make it through the surgery." I acknowledged what he said and immediately went numb. I closed my door, turned off the lights, and went to sleep.

Two weeks later, I was helping carry his casket to his final resting place. I was also asked - as I recall, by the presiding Chaplain at 5th SF Group - to deliver a eulogy.

Tribute to Pete

I didn't know how I was going to do that, so I asked God to give me words and the strength to get through it. Standing at the podium at the front of a large octagon-shaped memorial chapel, I breathed deeply and began. "It's an honor and privilege to be standing here today representing the ODA and the Special Forces community, and to be a witness of my brother Pete; to give an account of the man I saw and experienced. When we're put in the worst of circumstances we get to see who we truly are and what we're capable of.

"Special Forces Assessment and Selection attempts to choose its soldiers based on this idea. Their job is to put us through much so they can see who we truly are; if we have what it takes to respond to whatever commands come our way.

"I can personally confirm for you today that, in Pete, they truly found the best of the best – honorable, trustworthy, brave, courageous, and with an unshakable faith no matter the circumstances.

"As Pete deployed on his last mission for his country, I was struck by his own distinct kind of bravery and courage in the face of the unknown perils that would meet us that day. He knew our mission would bring us through enemy territory.

"The mission was simple and – like even routine assignments in the Iraqi theater – dangerous. But I had no doubt Pete would rise to whatever challenge it presented. He was more than just a soldier, he had something extra. He was all about the mission. Even though he had been tried by fire many times before being wounded less than a year prior, he was not hesitant in the least. Instinctively, he took the most dangerous position in the least defendable vehicle.

"In that, his final mission, Pete stood in the open turret strong and confident. He was ready for anything. Just his presence infused the rest of us with his courage.

"Within seconds after we hit the streets that day an IED exploded about four yards away. The results were catastrophic. I was wounded, and I knew Pete was, too. But he didn't cry or panic, in the cloud of confusion I could hear him, shouting out in anger at the enemy. He was trying to shake it off the effects of the blast, and of his injuries, and get back to the mission.

"The rest of us drew strength from his strength.

"Over the next few months, as I began my own recovery, I had the opportunity to visit Pete numerous times. And once again, it was he who was doing the inspiring. But it was this final mission for his country that Pete brought bravery, courage and honor to a whole new level. You see, I think in Pete's heart of hearts he knew that he was dying. Yet he spent all his remaining energy being strong for us and helping us along. He lasted as long as he could mentally and physically. And then, in his own unique and courageous way, he said goodbye, letting go.

"In many of my privileged moments with Pete, from Iraq to Walter Reed Hospital, I told him how proud the team and I were of him and how much he inspired me to be able to stay the course. He suffered, he endured, and never complained. To put it simply, he was my hero. I was also able to share with him that lives were now being saved because of the sacrifice he made on that fateful day. Army convoys would be done differently because of what they learned. I could tell that really meant a lot to him.

"I know so many of you prayed for Pete, some for his recovery, some simply for God's will to be done. I think those prayers were answered. Pete's not suffering anymore. That may sound trite; you may be asking yourself why people like Pete, good and noble, are wounded and die? I believe it's because life is a rare opportunity given us by a loving Father for just a splinter of time. In that tiny window,

He gives us a precious gift: free will. How we exercise that gift determines whether or not we will spend eternity in His company.

"It seems evident to me that, in the use of his gift, Pete learned discernment. He knew right from wrong, good from evil. He understood the impact his choices had on those around him. Ultimately, he learned self-sacrifice, and no gift costs so much, or comes with a greater reward.

Pete consciously chose good; to help, to offer his body as a living sacrifice so that others might live. He fully knew that serving in this way didn't guarantee a long life, quite the contrary – but if for God, his country, and the greater good, he'd put it all on the line to purchase a bright future for his children.

"This is Pete's legacy, and there's none nobler."

I felt compelled, somehow, to add the following: "And if you doubt a Creator exists – that Pete is truly in a better place – just look up to the heavens and the vast universe to know it is so. And if you look into your own heart you know it's true.

"Pete knew his Maker and had a relationship with Him. He took comfort in the prayers offered up on his behalf. More than once, I saw Pete's hand cover the hand of those that prayed for him in the name of Jesus. And he did not push it away or lie rigid in discomfort. Instead, he pulled in, held on, and in his heart trusted Jesus his Savior.

"I don't suppose many of us are comfortable with the thought of dying. Pete certainly didn't want to die – nor was he reckless with the life he'd been given – but he was completely at peace with death. Completely unafraid. Again, Pete continued to inspire me just like he had that day we mounted up for the mission.

"I am simply in awe of this young man. And look! He's still inspiring us. Right here, right now. So when you tuck your children in safe and sound tonight, know that it was

Pete – and other patriots like him – who gave their all to make that possible.

"Today we are honoring the life of a true hero. I don't know what else you could call him.

"Thank you, Buddy. I will miss you. But all of us who have established our relationship with God as you have done, will see you before long in that place, "that's got to be better than here." That perfect place where people suffer no more. And where finally we're able to take rest from our earthly journey. Where our Father will say, "Well done, my good and faithful servant."

"What else would Pete want to say? 'I love you, Caylee. I love you Terri and Mindy. I love you Grandma and Grandpa. Thank you all for allowing me to be part of your lives. May God hold you close and carry you all the days of your lives giving you peace, happiness and fond memories.'

"Pete, thank you for being the man you were, and the saint you've now become."

I saluted.

The service ended. The grieving family went home to figure out how to get their little ship back on course without its rudder. I went back to work on recovering from my own wounds. After the rest of the team returned from their eight-month combat tour to Mosul, we immediately began preparations for re-deployment.

My hand and arm regained some movement, but I had to use my other hand to assist with mostly everything. I still couldn't button a shirt or twist the cap off a water bottle, but I did learn to compensate with my other hand.

I did my best to hide the weakness and worked hard to make my fingers and hand do more. Everyone turned a blind eye to the disability and I returned to Iraq on that next deployment. As before, I volunteered to go as the advance party for the team. So off I went with basically one working hand and arm. It took years to regain complete use of them – meanwhile, the job was to make the most of what I had, as they were, and at the very least, learn how to keep them from getting in the way.

As the years went by, I grew very proud of the place I came to call home – 5th Special Forces Group. I suppose I started my journey with the military for all the wrong reasons; mostly, as you no doubt gather, I wanted to prove something to my dad. I think, too, I felt I needed to suffer so I could feel the punishment my dad said I deserved.

The mind is a strange thing.

There were so many reasons I needed the Special Forces.

In the final analysis, though, I had made myself useful to them, and the team came to rely on me and trust me as a valued member. I may have set out on the journey for all the wrong reasons, but I'd grown into my position as a functioning, integral part of something much bigger than myself.

We may have been Special Forces guys but we were also just broken units with something to prove. We matured

along the way and realized our country really did need us and was counting on us. Maybe many of us had unresolved issues but when you realize your country needs you to be bigger than those things your perspective changes – and they shrink to insignificance compared to saving people's lives. We were in the business of bringing people from the darkness of fear and oppression, into the light of freedom and hope, of getting medicine to people in dangerous places, and – at the same time – reminding hostile actors that, when attacked, America would retaliate. 5th Special Forces was sent to defend. Our mission included creating peace through strength.

We were knights in a world that needed them. My selfish motives to make my mark among the elite morphed into just wanting to serve, to prove worthy of people's trust to the point they would freely put their lives in my hands.

My new identity and occupation was *Defender*.

Looking back, I realize my upbringing prepared me for

life at the tip of the spear in the Special Operations community. The Army needed survivors, and that's what I was. With that raw material, Special Forces made me into something useful that could fulfill my role as defender – they made me a warrior.

From the time I rejoined the Army through 2004, my faith had subtly changed. In a way, it mirrored my military career – from raw recruit to Special Forces – spiritually, my journey of faith took me far beyond the comfort zone of my place in the pew. This, too, was a battlefield on which war was waged in a dimension Sun Su would never recognize. Here, I would only survive if I kept Jesus firmly in sight.

The more desperately I relied on him, the more deeply I rediscovered Him in a new, more personal way. From late 1995 through 2004, my faith was challenged and – just as a muscle only grows when set against an opposing force – it grew in ways I only recognize in retrospect. In any event, by the time I was wounded by the IED I had resolved to be a reflection of Christ to the world around me.

Spiritually, my time in the Army had been a journey through the wilderness. I was in a world completely separated from the loving arms of a home church. It was just Jesus, my Bible, and me. There wasn't the time, and only rarely the opportunity, to attend church. I was in a sea of worldliness. On occasion I would meet a Christian but for the most part I was alone in my faith.

I was determined not to fall away, but to press on, deeper into Jesus. As a result, I developed a kind of Christ-awareness – a depth of communion that I might never have experienced otherwise.

I talked with Him about everything. My Spirit groaned for His companionship. I maintained a constant conversation with Him in which I openly expressed my fears, my loneliness, my stress, my exhaustion, and my perceived want of courage. I felt a kinship of suffering; we both knew the wilderness – the weaknesses it reveals in us, the plague of temptation it unleashes on us.

Unlike Jesus, though, I often fell victim to temptation and deception.

However, over time I began to lean more on Him and less on my own understanding. I became both meeker and stronger, more humble, and more confident. Slowly my light began to emerge from under its bushel. My mannerisms reflected a quiet confidence, and my inner peace that resulted from that, began to impact those around me.

My relationship with Jesus had become so personal and intense that there were hardly any days I just prayed some distant prayer. My prayers were intense, needing, wanting, hoping at all times, in all circumstances for Jesus to get me through all the trials of being a Green Beret, of living a life that responded to danger by running toward it. Quite simply, I needed Him constantly. During that time, He ceased to be abstract. He became my Rock. My strength, shield, and salvation.

The Lord of my life.

Because of my growth in Him, I could handle the wounds, I could face death, and I could pray diligently and meaningfully for Pete. Even more importantly, I could accept God's sovereignty when, despite the prayers for Pete's family, his loved ones, his teammates, and I offered up on his behalf, he died. Ultimately, I could use the opportunity of delivering his eulogy to repeat God's message of salvation.

It may not have been a coincidence that I ended up at 5th Special Forces Group. Looking back, it's easy to see where God may have been using me. From 1995 to 2001 my teammates and I trained, lived, and worked together at my unit. We bonded during our many deployments that took us all over the Middle East. I was one Christian – one Green

Beret totally dependent on the Lord. I believe Jesus was with me. I believe He was protecting, assisting, guiding, blessing, giving grace, and living in our midst.

Chapter Nineteen

I trained the Pakistani Army and they, in turn, trained the Afghanistan resistance forces that would ultimately face down the Taliban.

In 1998 I was in Nairobi on deployment training the Kenyan defense forces and providing medical aid along the Somalia border 6 months before the embassy bombings and six months after. I was training the Yemen Army 6 months before the *USS Cole* attack. It seemed like I was always somewhere significant before, during or after international events occurred.

I stood on the trench line during Operation Desert Thunder on the Kuwaiti and Iraqi border ready to repel Saddam Hussein's latest threats to the world in 1999. My hundred man Special Forces unit was the first to be deployed to respond to the 9/11 attacks on the World Trade Center and Pentagon in 2001. My friend and barracks room neighbor was the first casualty in Afghanistan whose face was aired on CNN. Our unit lost four that day. They had a JDAM, a large guided bomb, mistakenly dropped on their position. They were killed by our own technology.

Friendly fire*.

My team inserted with the rest of the ODAs into the mountains of Afghanistan in October 2001. Subsequently, it was my team that chased Osama Bin Laden into the Mountains of Tora Bora. It was my team and the rest of the hundred-man force sent to Afghanistan who trained, fought, and ultimately defeated the Taliban, bringing freedom – however briefly – to the people of Afghanistan. It was my friend and teammate Kevin who became a saved, outspoken Christian on one of our last deployments before the 9/11 attacks.

I prayed constantly for my unit, my teammates and, specifically, for Kevin. That prayer was answered.

I don't imagine we struck anyone as a particularly holy-looking group as we went about our duties; whether we looked holy or not, but God was with us. I envisioned His having prepared my unit to be one of the arrows in his quiver in the fight against evil, and that we would be ready. In my mind, He lived and breathed and had His being through us. We were His chosen warriors to right the world. His blessings and grace were upon our efforts.

Those were my prayers, anyway. Who knows what difference my being there actually made? But the fact that I was there makes me believe I was right where He wanted me to be. In our weakness, He was strong.

September 11, 2003 Kevin was killed offering himself at the last minute to be the point man on a mission in Al Ramadi, Iraq. I had spoken with him just a day or two before. I don't recall if I prayed for him. I hope I did. Kevin had become one of my best friends on our twelve man-team; he was one of the first, if not *the* first, Special Forces casualty in the war starting in 2003 with Iraq and Operation Iraqi Freedom. I participated in his memorial service and funeral in Bald Knob, Arkansas. His wife Theresa became and continues to be a friend who I pray for and think about often.

Kevin's name is remembered today because God delights in using the things He makes His holy vessels. They have been blessed for purposes such as these and they have been sanctified to be used by God as He sees fit.

Several years ago the premiere training facility for the fight against terrorism was a base just outside the city of Kabul, Afghanistan. The mission of that critically important place was to protect both soldiers and citizens, to train troops for their battle with evil, and serve as a place of safety and sanctuary for those worn thin by that battle. It's named *Morehead Commando Training Center* after my friend: Kevin Morehead.

I won't pretend it wasn't a struggle to see God's Grand Design through all the suffering, death, and chaos happening around me. Was it all just a coincidence or had God had a specific plan all along? I was sure He had. I felt I was chosen; I'd been prepared for my role in all this, whatever that role might prove to be. However unholy I might be, He was using me.

I didn't process all this in real-time. Then – like everyone else – I was just reacting to events as they unfolded, as the orders and counter-orders rained down, trying to stay a half-step ahead of the situation just to survive, let alone be effective. I was simply in the throes of tough deployments, terrible tragedies, extremely stressful situations, and fearful circumstances.

But I'd chosen to be there.

Returning to Iraq had been a simple choice. I was a soldier and soldiering was all I knew. Truth is, I was more afraid of leaving the military than staying in and risking my life in combat. When the choice was made, I had to convince everyone around me – especially those above me – that I could perform to task despite my obvious physical injuries. I trained myself not to respond, in any visible way, to the shooting nerve pains in my hand and the constant aching in my elbow, where nuts and bolts from the IED were lodged permanently.

The right side of my face and tongue were somewhat numb and drooped, and my inner ear had been so badly damaged that all I could hear was a loud, high-pitched sound. I had to ignore it all if I was to function and be a useful team member.

In between my second and third combat tours, I was recommended for promotion to team warrant officer, one of the most respected position on the team. This is not a position you can apply for, the candidate has to be recommended by the Command. It was Command that chose me to become the team's gray-haired, unofficial subject matter expert.

After six months of warrant officer training, I returned to my team as a 180A, a Special Forces Warrant Officer.

By the time we returned to Iraq several months later, I, the new Warrant, just happened to be the guy our new team captain and new team sergeant would rely upon also. I was the technical leader for the team. In this capacity, it was my job – in part – to instill confidence in my unit about their upcoming mission. I was called "Chief", a mark of distinction. Additionally, the higher-ups in Special Forces leadership wanted to hear from their warrant officers. They wanted our thoughts and our recommendations. As the elders of the team, they trusted our instincts.

Many times the chief was put in charge of combat missions. Perhaps God used me to fight against evil and maybe He even used me to help change the tide of the war in Iraq. Probably not. Whatever the macro picture, in the micro He helped me locate, identify, and force ISIS from our area of operations in Iraq.

The notion of soldiers commuting back-and-forth to war strikes most people as odd. But that's warfare in the 21st Century. It's always been that way, really, though movies usually show soldiers fighting it out, surviving the odds and then going home at the end of it all. The behind-the-scenes footage remains on the cutting room floor, and is never talked about. I guess it would take away the romantic notions about soldiers being gone for years, then coming home to surprise their loved-ones.

In reality, soldiers come and go from war zones all the time. One minute you are searching bombed out buildings for body parts and weapons caches, the next you are flying home on Delta Airlines. Home by supper time to eat pizza with your family around the kitchen table. You are either home on leave or one of your family members has passed away. It could be that you finished your deployment and are back to normal garrison life. But in a few months, even though you put it out of your mind, you find yourself on a plane going back to pick up fighting the war where you left off.

Within eighteen hours mundane tasks like walking the dog, and taking out the trash can to your suburban curb seems like distant memories. You touch down under black out operations. Nothing has changed. Madonna music still blares and shuttles get you off the runway as soon as possible. You punch in and get back to work.

The long commute to Armageddon.

Just another day at the job. You feel embarrassed to recall that, not long ago, you knelt and kissed the tarmac when you deplaned in the States after your first deployment. It turns out, you didn't survive the war, you'd just survived a battle. How many of your nine lives had you used up?

And you're never home for good; you're just always gone, testing the limits of your luck or lack thereof, and the ever- decreasing odds of making it back out.

Normalizing a life that finds you driving through hostile territory in a Sun-baked desert – fully expecting the explosion or bullet that will end your life – at one moment, then hugging your kids, or watching Sunday Night Football with your neighbors the next, requires the kind of mental and emotional gymnastics that often leave a relatively sane person feeling detached and withdrawn.

The wife notices. "You've changed," she says.

I haven't changed. I'm the same guy, trying to stay sane.

The kids notice.

The soldier tosses a ball to his son and – when the ball is returned – flashes back to just a day or two before when some innocent-looking kid in an Iraqi village threw a live grenade at him in the same way. Dad doesn't catch the ball;

he ducks and dives. After a while, nobody talks about it. The pillow gets cold. The football gathers dust.

Chapter Twenty

Another Combat Tour in the Al Jazeera

Back on the job again, I adjust to the new normal. The day starts, as in most any office or job site in the western world, with a fresh pot of coffee. I've traded the sound of my wife reminding me to take out the trash and early-morning duty on the neighborhood leash brigade for squawking radios and heavy bullet proof kits.

After lacing up my boots and stretching out a bit with a yawn, I lock and load my M-4 and .45 caliber semi-automatic pistol, jump in our up-armored truck with the rest of the team, and we venture from the safety of the wire. One last look back at the shadowy figure manning the gate* to my temporary home.

Through my night vision goggles I observed the road ahead. The eerie green illumination, combined with the typical middle-eastern surroundings, cast ghostly silhouettes around me. Fences – strands of wadded up concertina wire braided with loosely strung barbed wire – line the sides of the road. Shredded plastic bags by the thousand festoon the fences and wave frantic farewells in the wind.

Large potholes, some filled haphazardly and others not, pock the broken asphalt ahead. Our Humvee proceeds slowly through the axle-breaking terrain, bumping and rocking. The driver, always alert to potential threats, slowly stitches the road with our zigzag tire tracks. The neighborhood passes in a blur – mud houses, abandoned store fronts, packs of barking dogs, and piles of garbage that seemed to dance on the sides of the road.

We sat within, looking like dark shadows. The glow from the computer screen reflected its low light onto my helmet and an assortment of red-green bulbs flickered for the numerous electronics crowding the interior. Wind swept through the vehicle from gunner's open turret. He stood scanning the road, sweeping the 50-caliber machine-gun, back and forth, from left to right locked positions.

I was overseeing an early morning patrol into the Al Jazeera region. Jazeera means desert in Arabic and we had recently increased our presence deep into its vastness. We brought our five Humvees to a predetermined intersection, stopped, and waited.

It was 0445 and the Iraqi force we were supposed to rendezvous with was late. In the moonless predawn, on an isolated stretch of city outskirts we waited like sitting ducks. Before long, a yellowish glow washed the horizon, soon followed by a steady stream of headlights. What I thought would be ten to fifteen vehicles turned out to be closer to fifty. Obviously, Lt. Ali, the commander in charge of the Iraqi force, thought he'd need extra help on our mission that day: intercept a probable high-level Al Qaida propaganda ministry meeting taking place in a remote desert village several kilometers away.

I was responsible for Lt. Ali and whomever he brought along – the one who would have to modify the plan and reorganize personnel to best suit the mission. I should have been in charge of roughly seventy-five soldiers. It was evident that I would now be in charge of approximately two hundred. It was a tall order and a big change. In Special Forces, the ability to adjust to unexpected situations comes with the territory. The policy for US support was always to allow the Iraqi forces to lead the way and "manage" the mission. However, it was the US forces that tactfully encouraged cooperation whereby the job got done.

Lt. Ali and another one of his blue and white police trucks would lead the way. My Humvee would be the second in line and the rest behind me. Eventually, the column of vehicles would stretch out over a half-mile. To minimize the likelihood of detection and avoid triggering the landmines lacing the road, Lt. Ali and I decided to drive deep into the desert and travel parallel to the highway until we reached the bridge at Tariq-Tariq Wadi.

Winding slowly and carefully, our long line of vehicles threaded around bushes, sand dunes, rocks, and washouts. The rough terrain ahead was only visible for as far as our black-out drive lights could penetrate the darkness. We carefully followed each turn and surrounding landscape features by utilizing our GPS computer screen.

After an hour, Lt. Ali started to stray off course. My Humvee took over the lead to steer the column back to the highway. Moving cross country, we reached the embankment about two kilometers before the bridge. A small village sat adjacent to the bridge and was the landmark that confirmed our exact location. Powering up the steep embankment, our Humvee scraped up and onto the road.

It was a good and bad feeling – Good that all the vehicles had made it, but bad that we were once more vulnerable to roadside bombs. The sun was rising over the eastern edge of the desert and an orange haze spanned our horizon. As the dew of a typical morning collected on our vehicle skins, small black birds became visible, darting across the sky. In the distance I could see the short hundred-foot, two-lane bridge. Also visible was the village. Wisps of smoke from the coal burning stoves rose into the sky and white goats and sheep grazed freely in the fields and courtyards.

Lt. Ali and his other vehicle moved in front of mine again and, as they reached the point where the village was to their immediate right, bullets hit, pinged, and thudded against our vehicles. "Contact right!" was echoed on the radio, then, "Contact left."

We were under attack. My instinct was to drive quickly through the buzzing enemy fire. The radios were jammed with voices screaming out direction of fire and commands. "Move, move, go, go, go!" Both sides of our vehicles were being hit with multiple weapons fire. We swerved our Humvee around Ali's vehicle and raced over the bridge, hopefully leading the convoy out of the kill zone.

On the other side, the paved road ended and open desert began. Those on the Iraqi radio frequency were having their own emotionally charged exchanges. It was verbal chaos in both English and Arabic. The concern was greater for the Iraqis in their lighter armored police vehicles. Directly on top of the Tariq-Tariq bridge, the thought flashed through my mind that it might be wired with explosives. Instead, more intense enemy fire occurred. Hammer-like thuds against the left and right side doors pelted us over and over from the wadi and elsewhere. Our thick bulletproof windows started spidering with other thuds, ricochets, and pings.

RPGs would be next, I thought.

From behind us, I could hear our teammates returning fire with machine-guns. My own gunner returned 50 cal bursts, spitting red-hot brass casings into the compartment, clanging loudly onto the floorboards around our feet. With the opening first burst my ears rang and muted all other sounds around me. My head and eyes seemed to vibrate with every concussion from above.

Heavier, more direct automatic enemy fire awaited us after we crossed the bridge, hitting our windows and steel with the force of a hundred sledge hammers. We had driven into a three pronged ambush with the enemy to our left, right, and front.

Eight inches from my nose, my windshield absorbed a massive bullet strike. Had it penetrated, the bullet would have gone straight between my eyes. I swallowed hard and took a deep breath. Not sure if there were snipers or just blistering concentrated fire, I didn't spend much time contemplating the matter.

To my surprise, the enemy didn't close in behind us; It was just Lt. Ali's vehicle and ours. He was completely pinned down – a sitting duck. I thought of the RPGs again, but pushed the thought away. I attempted to call the others to rally on our Humvee location, but because of the surprise of the situation everyone either forgot to turn off their radio frequency jamming, or the enemy force was jamming it for us. Either way, I needed another plan and quickly.

I surveyed the battlefield ahead. The desert was flat with ridges and vehicle tracks fingering off in all directions. The tracks all led up a modest incline to a slight but strategic elevation. Further ridges beyond leapfrogged each other and staggered off to the horizon.

The well-camouflaged enemy positions could be anywhere and more traps, standard to insurgent techniques, were probably ahead. The personnel behind me probably didn't realize the wall of lead awaiting them on my side of the bridge. I ordered my Humvee to turn around and signaled Ali to follow. I had to get the lighter-skinned Iraqi trucks to safety and out of the range of the RPGs that were sure to come. Crossing back across the bridge, I motioned everyone to get on-line facing the enemy in front of the wadi.

Just then I saw the entire Iraqi force had pulled over and stopped off to the side of the road using the berm for cover. I raced back to them. The Iraqis were hunched down, some under their vehicles, behind the open doors, or hunkered down inside the cabs, still taking harassing fire which was not as intense, but still a threat.

Through my interpreter Elvis, nicknamed for his sideburns and sunglasses, we split and reorganized their forces and ordered them to clear the adjacent village and secure it.

After this, from two-hundred-meters away, I saw our ODA, a few of Ali's, and two attached U.S. support vehicles now on the other side of the bridge. An Iraqi vehicle was tipped into the wadi as if they had attempted to cross. The scene was bizarre; nearby a Humvee was being pelted with heavy machinegun fire as its driver dodged this way and that in search of cover. In the open, men ran in whichever direction instinct told them offered the best protection, tossing themselves behind berms, the bridge's concrete columns, anything that would provide enough protection so they could return fire. Smoke grenades exploded all around, adding a surreal, other-worldliness to the chaos.

They were in the heart of the kill zone. Worse yet, they were trapped by those of their own vehicles blocking the bridge behind them. I analyzed the situation in an instant and raced our vehicle back into the fight.

In the process, I was able to get through to some of the other drivers to move forward and, within a minute or two, the rest of the Humvees were finally on-line and had formed a semi-circle on the far side of the bridge to return fire. The enemy was out in the desert determined to keep us from crossing. We were equally determined to take it.

Initial position of friendly and enemy forces.

EVENT 1: Immediately after crossing Sukariyah bridge SFOD-A, ESU, B/1/3 IN and ERU were engaged from numerous directions with MG, RPG, SAF, IDF and two sniping elements.

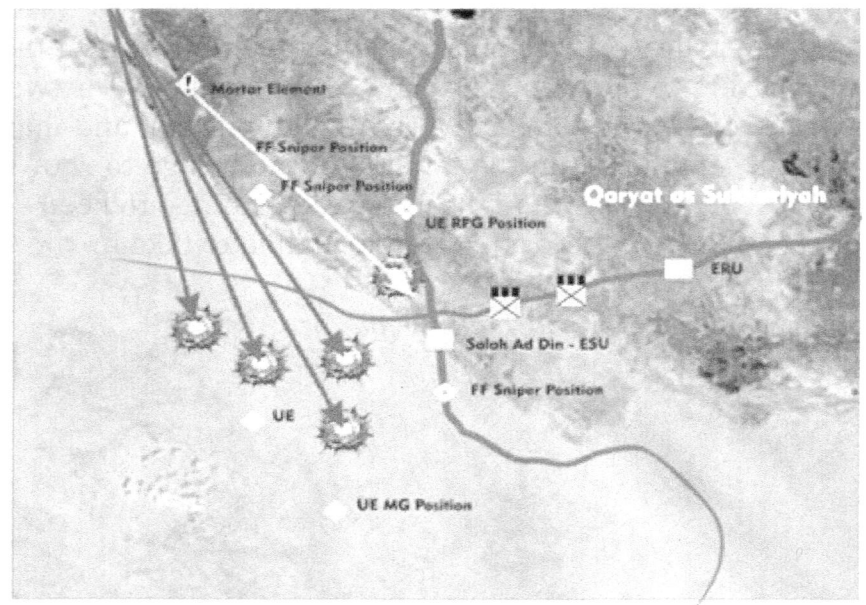

Mortar Element

FF Sniper Position

FF Sniper Position

UE RPG Position

Qaryat as Subayriyah

ERU

Saloh Ad Din - ESU

FF Sniper Position

UE

UE MG Position

EVENT 2: A mortar element engaged the front line trace of the patrol with 3-5 IDF size unknown.

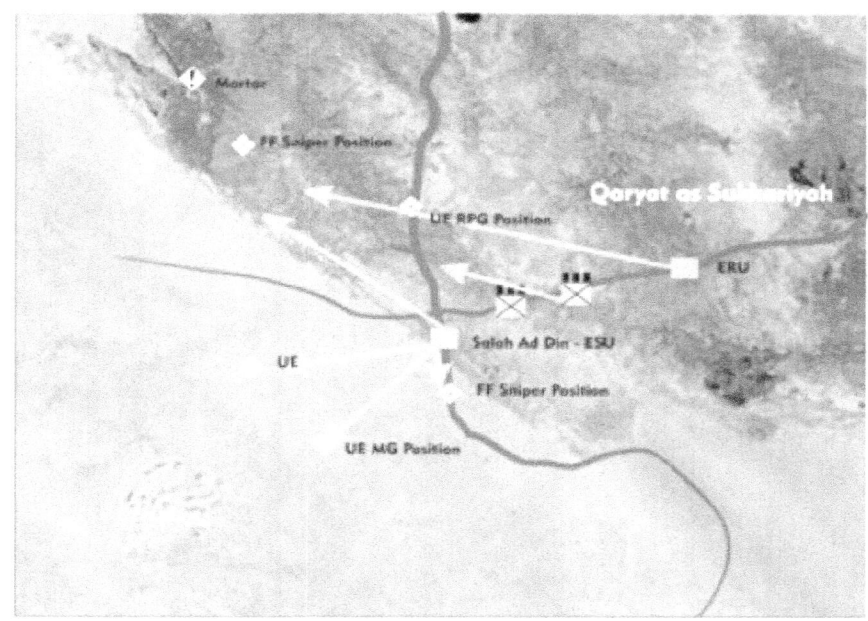

EVENT 3: All Friendly elements returned fire and maneuvered to more advantageous positions.

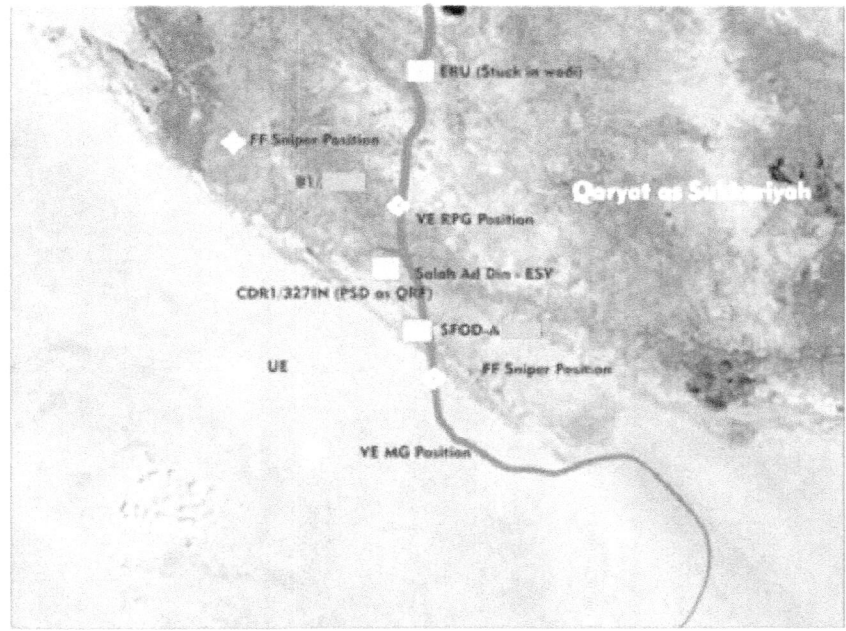

EVENT 4: SFOD-A moved forward to support trapped ESU element.

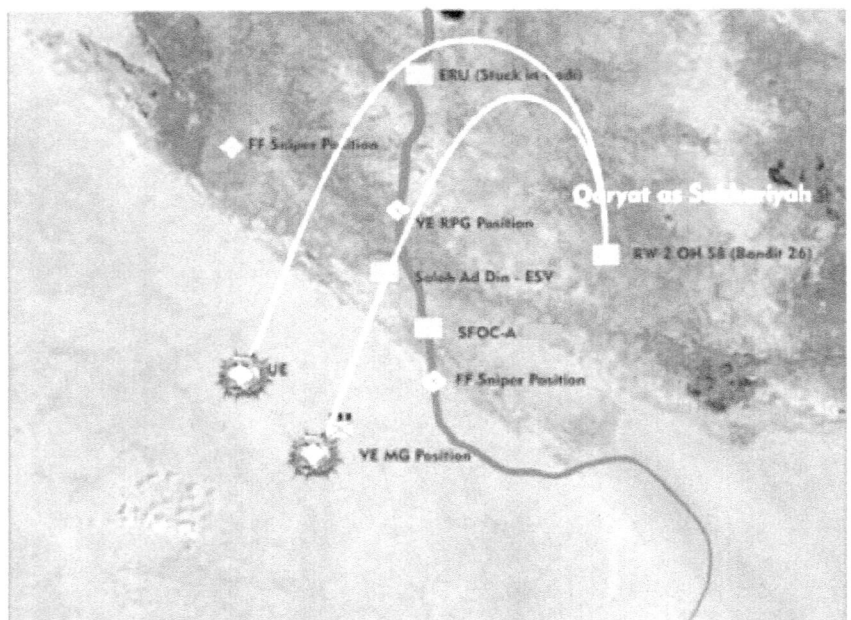

EVENT 5: 1 section OH-58s arrive on station and engage MG/RPG position with 2.75mm rockets.

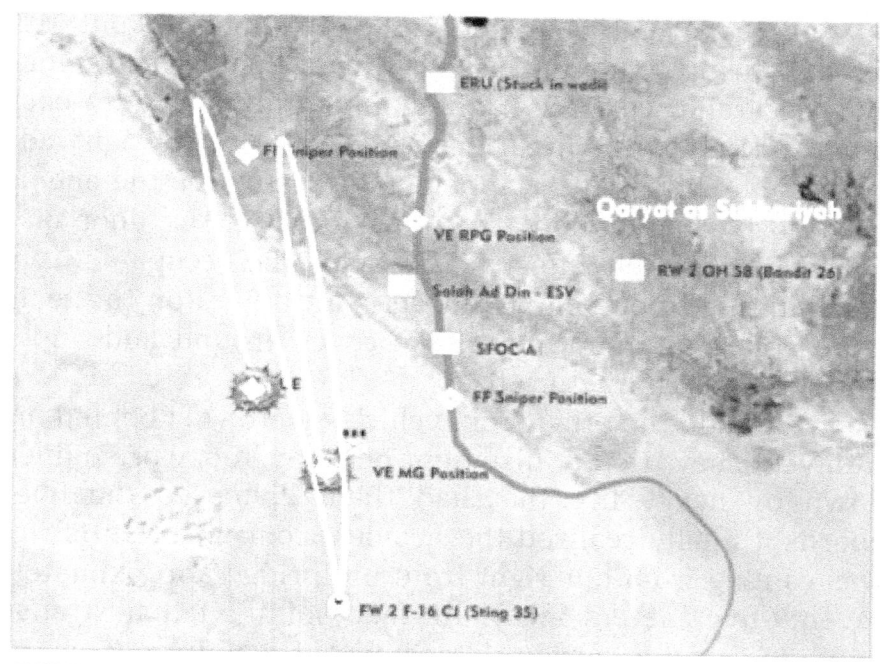

EVENT 6: FW section engages MG/RPG position with 20mm guns.

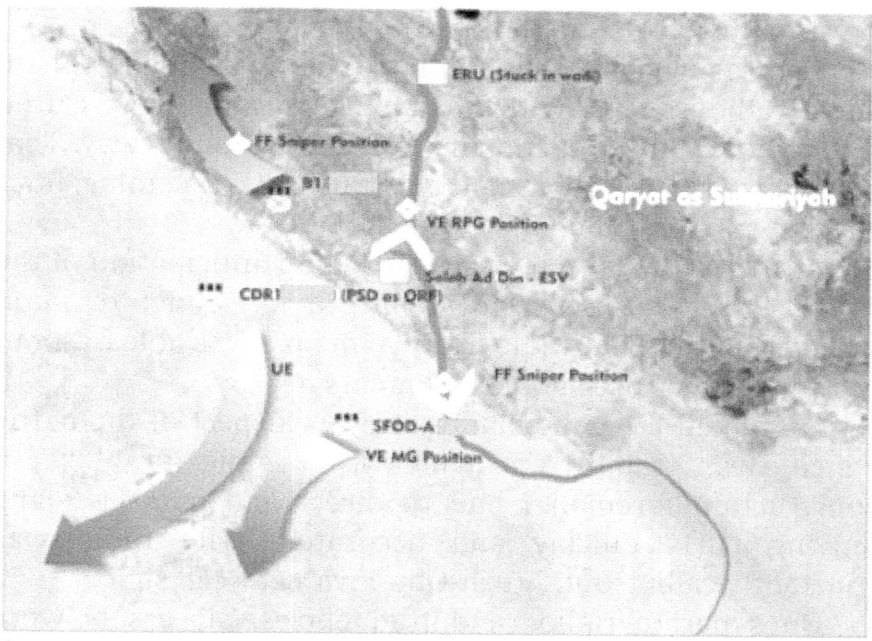

EVENT 7: All elements converged on enemy positions and cleared enemy forces.

Several 50 Cals, M-60 machine-guns, M249s and M4s were all firing simultaneously. It was deafening. The smoke was thick and we were running ammunition cans to each other to keep up the fire. Our Humvee was to the right side of the semi circle. As it happened, that is where the enemy was most concentrated. They had targeted the door of a Humvee to our left, effectively keeping the occupants from dismounting to personally engage. But others on the team were able to scramble out, take cover around and under their vehicles, and return fire.

Lt. Ali and the other Iraqi vehicles were well behind my Humvee. They tried to dismount but they, too, were pinned down by heavy fire that had them diving to the floor boards. I finally realized the heaviest concentration of fire was coming from our right front on a ridge approximately seventy-five meters away. At that point I felt a strange numbness and a certain detachment. I was furious at the failure of radio communications, something that should *never* happen to soldiers in the field.

Before our dash back into the fight, I was finally able to make radio contact with headquarters, and was assured that a QRF –Quick Reactionary Force – was on its way. That meant several heavily armed gun trucks were coming, but I was not sure how long that would take.

Also gnawing at me was the nagging anticipation of the RPG rounds that I figured would hit us sooner or later. Although I could not radio my own team, I was able to shout commands to those support elements nearby.

It seemed I was in charge of every aspect of the battle which was rapidly growing in complexity. Like a construction foreman I had to direct and manage many moving parts quickly and accurately. The radio was constantly calling out, "Rush-One-Five", our call sign.

On separate radios and frequencies, air assets were advising they were "on station" wanting a situation report and guidance. Attack helicopters – acting on tactical information we provided – made runs up and down Tariq-Tariq Wadi firing mini guns, reporting movements and requesting instructions. They banked low overhead and fired rockets at the enemy position on the ridge; mini-gun fire that swept from one side to the other. Geysers of sand and dirt shot up as the rounds hit the ground.

I was out of my vehicle with a weapon in one hand and a radio mike to my ear with the other. I quickly surveyed the sky and had to scream over the continuous machine-gun fire, jet, and helicopter noise. As the scene got more intense the pilot of the F-16 was calm and steady. From his end all I heard was the low whine of his engine. From my end, he got an earful of explosions, automatic weapons fire, and men yelling back and forth.

As soon as the desperation of the situation hit home, the pilot immediately joined the tempo of the fight and came screaming in. Because of the relative proximity of the combatants, the pilot had difficulty differentiating our team's location from that of the enemy. From my Humvee we threw smoke grenades towards the enemy's positions but the pilot still thought it too "danger close."

I then noticed something out of the corner of my eye: muzzle flashes off in the distance to my right flank. Enemy forces were out in the desert taking careful aim and firing single shots one after another. I couldn't hear the shots coming to tear into my body but I could count the milliseconds each one would have taken to hit. It was odd and interesting all at the same time. I could see the rounds being fired at me but the flashes I saw didn't compute. If I couldn't hear them, they didn't seem as real or deadly somehow.

The bullet never came.

Chapter Twenty-One

I turned my attention to the scene unfolding before my eyes. As the situation became increasingly more confusing and intense, my Soul became quieter. As I had learned in SF schools, the body has a way of turning off everything that's unimportant to focus on a single action. Everything slows down, sounds are muffled and yet instincts stay intensely sharp. I wasn't more courageous than anyone else, my survival mechanisms were just working at peak instinctual levels.

I was all but deaf except for the ringing in my ears from the prolonged weapons fire. One of the Iraqi Humvees suddenly sped past to my right and slid to a stop in a cloud of dust about fifty meters away, a position atop a knoll from which they could strafe the enemy position, which they did, and fiercely. Their targets were on the other side of the knoll, beyond my line of sight.

As I watched, I radioed the F-16 to conduct a strike on that general area. I ran over to a nearby Humvees and told them to drive to the Iraqi location on the knoll and get them to fall back so they'd be out of harm's way when the jet made its pass.

By then, the Iraqi gunner had run out of ammunition and was standing in his turret defiant and completely exposed. I fully expected him to be torn to shreds by enemy fire at any second, but some slight motion forward caught my eye and redirected my attention; an RPG round, then another, and finally a third ripped through the sky, slammed into the ground, skipped through the dirt sending up showers of dust and debris, and settled finally to a stop just five meters from me, each one a little closer than the one before.

Despite all my training, I was transfixed. This was it. There was absolutely nothing I could do. I don't know if I said, "Lord, forgive me my sins. Here I come!" but I felt it.

But the explosions didn't come. Bending low, I scurried closer to the nearest bomb and saw that the tape holding its safety pin in position was still in place. It would never explode that way. The same was true of the other two. The enemy, in their haste had forgotten to remove the tape and safety pins. Still, instinctively, I shouted, "RPGs!" but no one could hear me.

I wondered if there would be more. If so, I was sure the enemy would have realized their mistake and armed the bombs. Attack helicopters swept in from the east, firing their mini guns, and my attention was yanked back to the right flank and the situation with the Iraqi Humvee. The RPG problem would have to wait.

The Humvee I had sent to warn the Iraqis roared back, skidding to a stop at my driver's side door. At the same time the F-16 requested permission to provide a "show of force" maneuver, which I gave. He made a low pass, close and thunderously fast, but it seemed to have no effect on the enemy.

All my senses were strained as I watched the jet lift off the deck and dart straight up out of sight. Continuous weapons fire, radio chatter and yelling in multiple languages assaulted my ears as my eyes burned and I choked on a cocktail of carbon, smoke, and dirt. Our Iraqi allies were dragging the limp body of a fallen comrade from their vehicle. They laid him on the ground at my feet. Crying and wailing, they knelt beside him and threw fistfuls of dust into the air in a show of mourning.

I recognized the defiant gunner; he'd been shot in the head.

Our driver, who was also the team medic, dismounted and started to work on the Iraqi, refusing my offer to help. The loud mourning of the Iraqi's comrades was drawing attention to our position and enemy rounds began to shower down upon us.

I shouted, pointing at the approaching columns of dirt spitting up as the enemy gauged our distance. The medic snapped angrily at the Iraqis to stop their mourning ritual but either they didn't understand or were so overcome by the depth of their loss they'd lost their senses. Little eruptions of dirt traced a pattern toward our vehicle and ricochets pinged off the ground and wheel wells. The medic dragged the injured man between the vehicles for cover. I rushed to his side. If nothing else, I could provide up-close communication with the medic, wave off the other soldiers, and scan for the location of the incoming fire. I knew that being there mattered. Just then, I heard "Rush-One-Five, Rush-One-Five."

I jumped back on the radio and leaned in the driver's side as far as I could to see what the medic was doing. The gunner's brain matter oozed from the top of his forehead where the round had entered. His eyes were open but glazed over. It was at that moment the medic lifted his eyes to meet mine. Knowing what he needed to hear, I made eye contact with him. "Let him go," I said.

I knew the command ran counter to the medic's instinct and training, but I had to make it. He was one of only three men defending our position.

Death didn't come to that soldier like it does in the movies, where the fallen hero delivers a little speech, takes a few neat breaths, and expires in his buddy's arms to the accompaniment of heroic music. No. The Iraqi soldier was dead, but his body hadn't gotten the message yet. Decisions like the one I had made were hard, but if unnecessary casualties were to be avoided they had to be made.

As he gathered his stuff together I mouthed the same platitudes I'd heard before, and received with such disdain: "It's not your fault," and "We told them to get out of there." Etc., etc. Blah, blah, blah. I knew, in the long run, the medic would not be consoled by that. It is not the way they are wired.

Maybe the Army should give more courses in battlefield triage.

Three Quick Reactionary Force trucks suddenly pulled up, and, as if he was delivering his team to a firing range for some refresher training, the base commander climbed out and his men followed. I, somewhat bemused, convened with him at the back of the vehicle, trying to mirror his casual attitude. Instinct told me I should crouch, but at the same time I felt I had to show myself equally "brave". In the background, the machine gun fire stitched the atmosphere. "Ta-ta-ta-ta-ta...baa-baa-baa-baa!"

"So, what's the situation?" the commander asked loudly.

Bullets slammed toward us in neat rows. We ducked behind my Humvee where, shouting above the din, I brought him up to speed. I waited for him to take over the operation. In my mind, that made perfect sense. After all, as an infantry battalion commander, not only did he outrank me, he was far more experienced and competent, and a great leader.

To my surprise, he just said, "Where do you need us?" Evidently, I was still in charge. Amazed and amused, but with no time to reflect on it I decided that what I needed more than anything at that moment was someone I could communicate with on my extreme right flank, my blind spot. I asked him to take the QRF and secure that position. He did.

All the chaos, jammed communications, and many moving parts to the adrenaline-fueled combat situation made repositioning entire U.S. formations of personnel and equipment impossible – pretty much the normal leadership challenge when under attack. With all the air-support temporarily off-station, I wanted to move each vehicle, in intervals, with radio coordination, through the entire suspected battlefield. Without being able to physically see every enemy position, the only way to find and neutralize them was to move forward and fight through them.

Some time had passed since the rounds of RPGs, I dared hope there'd be no more danger from that quarter and, if there were, maybe they, too, would have taped safety-pins.

You can always hope.

In any event, once the commander was in position, everything went into motion and the odds began to tilt slowly in our favor. I moved my Humvee about twenty meters and then signaled for the QRF to do the same. I repeated the steps on my left and right, back and forth. The other vehicles followed suit. Turret gunners fired, clearing hills and ridge tops to their immediate fronts.

As anticipated, the QRF ran into the concentrated enemy fire to the right. I trusted the Commander to clear that threat and ordered the main force forward.

Radio communication was sporadic, with bits and pieces of information breaking through the static like electronic shrapnel. Still, it was enough to give me a fairly good pic-

ture of the overall situation. I ordered the advance. For another kilometer we leap-frogged across the ridged terrain. I then turned the entire formation, wheeling it right.

A few mud and mortar-structured villages needed to be cleared in the distance. The commander would take the nearest village closest to the right and I, with the other trucks, would race across the now flat and dusty desert to the second.

The sight of a phalanx of combat vehicles on-line, (side-by-side, parallel, in a line, or abreast of one another, in formation) sending dust skyward as they advanced at speed across the desert floor was, to me, impressive. For our opponent, it would have been terrifying. We rapidly closed the distance on the villages.

Off to my right, I saw the flank vehicles reach their village. All the trucks and Humvees were on-line – bringing to mind a charge of Patton's 3rd as his tanks swept across northern France – making their way side by side past the commander's village position. It was a picture-perfect maneuver. Patton would have approved.

Making a quick turn-around after a sweep of the small village, word reached me that I was needed at the QRF's new position. There are often instances in combat where there is not enough information to even be able to guess what someone else's situation might be. To me, considering the events of the day thus far, that radio call could have meant anything. The tone in the voice, however, hinted that no real hurry was required. It sounded more like someone needed to talk face-to-face.

When I arrived at the QRF's village, soldiers and Iraqi police forces were running around and maneuvering their trucks in ordered chaos, in the middle of which the commander stood waiting for me.

The commander was clearly upset. "Sir," I started, indicating Ali's forces with a nod, "They do things their own way here. We just advise. For them terror is part of their psychological warfare. They're sending a message to the enemy out here in the desert, a message intended to strike fear into the enemy – not us."

The commander shook his head. "Are we done here, Chief?"

"Yes, Sir."

I thanked him and his team for pulling us out of the fire. Returning to my Humvee I surveyed the scene through the windshield. While our work would never make the textbooks, we'd won through with minimal casualties – despite the fierceness of the encounter. Ali's reputation for showing strength and tactical ability was bolstered; word of it would sweep through towns and villages. Perhaps insurgents would think twice before testing his mettle.

His reputation, and that of others like him, contributed in large part to our protection against future attacks from IEDs, snipers, or other ambushes. We were safer if we had units like Ali's on our side. Alone, we'd have been at the *mercy* of units like his. Better to make them our ally than another enemy.

Later in the day, various elements reported their status and location by radio. Back at the ambush sight I watched all the military personnel loitering about, creating a circus-like atmosphere. The Iraqis danced traditional dances with their arms linked to form a circle, celebrating their victory with well-known Arabic songs. The junction looked like a parking lot, but without a single vehicle in its appointed slot. Disorder prevailed with blue and white pickup trucks, tan Humvees, large cargo vehicles, and even cars massed in no particular order.

Some walked about in small, animated groups or ming-

led with others, their hands in constant motion as, with weapons slung from their shoulders, they recounted their heroics. Captured enemy suspects had been rounded up for transportation and further questioning.

Assembled around another white pickup truck, several more Iraqis laughed and took pictures. Six mangled bodies were in the bed of the truck, stacked like floppy rag dolls, all in civilian clothing. Their shredded clothes hung off them like horrific Halloween costumes. Blood swished side-to-side in the bed of the truck, flies stuck in the already-matted long, bloody hair. Jagged bullet holes had caused compound fractures and shattered faces. The head of one combatant with long purple hair was half blown away.

As the Iraqis tried to sit the body up for an identification photograph, his brains spilled over the jagged edge of his skull. One of the Iraqi soldiers caught them and tried, unsuccessfully, to stuff them back into the head.

In the surreal fog of the aftermath, I observed that, from

the other side, he looked like someone sleeping peacefully.

While I understood, I couldn't remain and watch. I walked away before the rest of the bodies were photographed for the reports.

For the first time that day I surveyed the battlefield in its entirety. I saw it all much more clearer than before. To my right was the wadi and low ridge from which the opening salvos had come. The battle replayed in my mind. What could I have done differently? How could I gather better intel? What needed to be done to make electronic communication flawless? How could I have used my resources to greater effect?

The leader of the bomb EOD (Explosives Ordnance Disposal unit*) called out to me after I passed the bridge, "Hey, just thought you'd want to know, we found explosives under the bridge. The blasting caps detonated but they must have been jerked out of the main charge somehow. Otherwise you'd all have been blown to hell." That was their plan.

"We also found a few RPG rounds up there and they . . ." I cut him off. "I know. I saw the tape and pins." I was suddenly exhausted. I grunted in acknowledgment of his efforts, took one last look at all the revelry and walked back to my vehicle. I accepted that it was what it was. We had seen it all that day. Then I heard the muffled, scratchy radio call out one last time, "Rush One-Five, Rush One-Five, can we get a sitrep?" This was a request for an update on our operation and status.

My Review of Combat

I was an explosives and demolitions expert within Special Forces. Altogether I served twenty-nine years in the Army, twenty-two mainly on a combat dive operational detachment, with more than eighteen deployments to semi-permissive, non-permissive* and combat environments throughout the Middle East. I taught other soldiers, both U.S. and allied forces, how to employ deadly devices in unconventional and irregular warfare. Our targets were everything from bridges, roads, trains, dams, and power-stations, to booby-trapped desk drawers rigged to explode when opened.

I taught them how to take apart shoulder-fired rockets and use them as improvised bombs; the art of guerilla warfare and tactics was my job. It was all justified because I was equipping oppressed people to free themselves from tyranny. Even our noble motto was *De Oppresso Liber: Freedom For The Oppressed.*

As I trained, advised, and assisted others in the art of killing and destruction, I saw myself as a Christian warrior protecting the world from evil. In truth, though, I wasn't so much defeating evil as absorbing it. Perhaps I was even perpetuating it. My faith suffered and my relationship with my Savior had been eroded.

His message was the Good News of salvation, of peace and love. That was not the message I was carrying into the world.

War is Satan's amusement park, a place where everything is upside-down and backwards, where violence and death not only predominate, they're celebrated. There's no place for the Ten Commandments here. Morality is one of the first things to die in this harsh landscape and the absolutes of right and wrong shrink to insignificance.

Anything can be justified if you try hard enough.

What happens to the individual soul in a world where love and compassion have no place? The heart hardens. Cynicism sets in and runs deep, seizing conscience in a stranglehold that deadens it to suffering.

I can't pretend to know the images that play across the minds of most men when they close their eyes to sleep. I only know what I see.

I see war; a place where caring is a luxury you can't afford. Where you don't give a thought to the thud under your wheels as you cross a village square. Was it a dog, or something else? I remember being annoyed by the constant rat-a-tat hammering from the next tent as yet another coffin was nailed shut. I was trying to write a report.

I see an old man leaning against a cinder-block wall waiting to die because that is how you do it there. Another staggering across the street, arms outstretched in supplication; he's been shot. Some people laugh, some look away, others don't even register the event as he falls into the dirt and breathes his last.

I see a disembodied face staring up at me from the dirt, the mask of death. I see a little family attempting to carry on living life in a second-floor apartment the walls of which have been blown away.

I see a kid with pink and orange hair, probably from the U.K. – lured to the Middle East by enemy propaganda – lying dead atop a heap of rubble. I see Iraqi soldiers standing in line, smoking cigarettes, chatting and laughing among themselves as they seem to wait their turn to have a word with an enemy combatant.

The look in the eye of the man who risked everything to come speak with you in hopes you can do something to save his home, his family. He'll be killed as soon as he leaves your little bubble of protection, and you both know it. You just stare at him until he goes away to meet that fate.

I see a truck engine sitting in the remains of a living room where it landed after a recent blast. Children make it part of their play. I see my buddy squatting over an ammo can because he can't hold the nervous bowels as white-hot

50 caliber ammo casings rain down on his head inside the Humvee. I see the curious calm and peace in a dead man's face as I take cover behind his body; a few more bullets won't hurt him. For a moment, I envy him – a doctor, if his crisp white gown is anything to go by. and the beautiful blood spattered patterns.

I smell the nauseating miasma of blood swishing around in the back of pick-up trucks. I see a hand still gripping tight to a steering wheel of the truck a suicide bomber drove into a barricade. Just the hand. The rest of him, I'm sure, is scattered about.

I relive those three RPG rounds that skidded to a stop just a few feet away. This time there is no tape. No pin.

I see those Iraqi soldiers mourning the death of their friend, flinging dirt into the air and wailing – oblivious to the enemy fire tearing into the earth all around them – with no other purpose than to turn them from mourners into victims in an instant.

I hear the deafening roar of your turret gunners returning fire. Hear the calm, almost detached chatter of the fighter pilot on the radio as he maneuvers his craft into position above the field of battle. I wonder if, in some way, he envies those of us engaged in battle on the ground, or if he's content to sweep in an out of harm's way at almost the speed of sound, strapped tightly into his leather throne. One second he's there, sowing devastating and somewhat random destruction, the next – he was miles away.

I see the veining of the windshield five inches from my face as, one after the other in endless array, sniper's bullets test the strength of that transparent defense with the impact of a sledge hammer. It's only glorified glass and plastic, after all.

Once again, I see forests of shredded plastic bags skewered to branches, bushes, and barbed wire. This is foliage that knows no season. It just flutters in the wind, waving good-bye to the souls of the dead.

So many dead. So many souls. So many plastic bags waving the only farewell those dead will ever know.

I hear the battlefield surgeon complaining how foul my breath is – the result of the blood coagulating in my mouth. He demands my blood type and I gurgle a reply.

I see the chaplain secretly take cans of beer at the commissary and stuff them into his backpack – liquid reinforcement to his faith so he can face one more day in in the death camps of combat.

These are the things I see when I close my eyes. Very likely, if your husband, or son, father, or uncle was a soldier in any military engagement since World War II, they have their own little theater of horrors in which similar memories play over and over again – a war with no treaty, and no end in sight.

Inevitably, I became desensitized to inhumanity – had I not, I'd have been crushed by its cruelty. I didn't even flinch anymore when explosions fell around the huts, I was writing an e-mail or watching a show and couldn't be bothered. Besides, I was convinced I'd know the sound of the missile that had my name on it when it came. For some reason, I imagined I'd have two seconds to say a prayer and beg forgiveness. I'd rehearsed that prayer.

For all my grand intentions, this is what I'd become. The intentions remained, though. I still wanted to help *the least of these* everywhere. But that would require more than just obedience to Christ's command, it needed love, and I'd become incapable of that, and only God could supply it.

Chapter Twenty-Two

A Spiritual Lesson in PTSD

From my early days of deployment to the IED that sent me home in 2004, through 2007, explosives were my life; I was either planning their placement and setting them off, or defending against them. One day I might be assigned to blow up a bridge or train track, the next to nullify enemy caches – piles of mortar and artillery rounds, possibly booby-trapped.

Left unsaid was the fact that I was of no use dead. So simple survival was top priority, and I got good at it. I survived the firefight in the desert. I survived encounters with multiple enemy combatants. I survived the IED that killed Pete. I survived my father.

I survived until 2010 when, in Baghdad, I served as an advisor to Iraqi special forces high command. In that capacity, I traveled the country.

I had served in four combat rotations; OIF II, IV, VII, and

X.

Over that time I learned a lesson; survival of the body does not mean survival of the human being. In the end, I was broken, a shell of the man I had been. Finally my mind completely collapsed. I had shut down. I could no longer keep to a train of thought; I couldn't even finish a prayer in my head. My whole being was trapped in panic mode twenty-four hours a day; my reaction to even the slightest unexpected stimulus was fight, flight, or freeze. It felt like my blood had been replaced by a volatile compound of adrenaline and TNT that absorbed all the energy by body could generate. I was a biological lighthouse of hyper vigilance and paranoia.

Returning to the U.S. and Fort Campbell, I received a medical retirement from the military. It quickly became evident that, while I could dress my body in civvies, my psyche was in fatigues. The most benign stimulus triggered a battlefield response. I'll leave it to you to imagine – based upon the foregoing – what went through my mind when I saw people standing in a line, glanced into the bed of a pickup truck, heard a roofing crew hammering shingles into place, the sound of dogs barking, a peal of thunder, or caught light glancing from a window or mirror.

For months, I lay in bed, cutting myself off from everybody and everything. I hunkered down in the back of my room where nothing moved unexpectedly, where there were no unfamiliar noises. From that tiny perspective I could maintain control of my environment. It was a desperate attempt to quiet my frayed nerves.

I was soon diagnosed with Post Traumatic Stress Disorder (PTSD) and prescribed several psychiatric medications. I took them all. I participated in various forms of counseling and therapy. I tried to claw my way back into normal life a little at a time, but the harder I tried, the lonelier and more isolated I felt.

The familiar words from the movie I so idolized, that once inspired me but I had never fully grasped, I now understood. John Rambo, breaking under the weight of his PTSD, struggled to explain: "You just don't turn it off! Back here there's nothing! I can't even hold a job parking cars. I've been doing this for seven years. Every day I have this. I don't talk to anyone, sometimes a day – a week I can't put it out of my mind. Where did everybody go?"

In my quest to become the heroic John Rambo, I had become the broken John Rambo. Within a few years, I was driven once more to my knees – confessing my sins and begging forgiveness – but the peace I longed for didn't come. Not that forgiveness wasn't given – I was simply so overcome by shame and guilt that I couldn't receive it.

In truth, I can't say all the wounds are completely healed, even now, and – like the 'thorn' in Paul's side, I might take them to the grave. The good news, perhaps the best I can hope for, is that I'm no longer incapacitated by them. I've learned to live with them. Maybe the grace that leaves you struggling against your demons, fighting the good fight, constantly building your spiritual muscles while, at the same time, drawing all your strength from the Savior, is the greater grace. After all, I didn't become a Green Beret by sitting back and hoping events would unfold in my favor. I challenged every atom of my being, day-after-day, until long past my natural breaking point.

Why should I expect my spiritual training in the battlefield of life to be any less rigorous? Muscles – whether physical or spiritual – only grow when pitted against opposing forces.

In time, I came full circle, and was able to reclaim my original calling as a Christian, my God-ordained purpose. I became aware that, whether or not I ever found that peace or joy, the only thing that would give me any sense of purpose would be serving the Lord. The question was, how? What had all my life experience equipped me for? What did He want me to do?

Of all the counsel I received on those issues, the best was the simplest: 'Begin the day by asking the Lord what He wants you do with the next few hours, then listen. Watch and wait. If nothing particular presents itself, you can't go wrong by simply following His commandment: take the Gospel to the world. Isn't that what being born again is all about?'

If I had to do it all over again, I would not take for granted the sweet relationship that once seemed so easy and possible. I would stay close by His side, throw away my pride, and live by the Spirit.

One day, while on my knees, praying, I was reminded of a scene from a nature program I'd watched: a sheep lay on its back, staring blankly at the sky. I'd seen faces like that in

Iraq. I'd been the man behind such a face, once. I imagined its blurred vision, the high-pitched ringing in its ears, its dizziness, exhaustion, confusion – and helplessness.

In the program, the shepherd lifted the animal to its feet, but its legs were numb, so it fell over again. It's called being 'cast down'. It's a not-uncommon condition, and a truly pathetic sight. In that flash of prayerful contemplation I understood a metaphor. The sheep is alone, its wool coat – representing the burden of sin – is too much to bear. It falls under the weight of it and can't get back up. Without help its legs go numb, and it begins to die upside down, its eyes wide but unseeing. Only the shepherd can get the sheep back on its feet, and hold it there until it has the strength and presence of mind to stand on its own.

The Shepherd – *my* Shepherd – is Jesus. I may have had Him on my mind the whole time, but subconsciously I kept Him at arm's length. I'd wandered the fringes of my faith for too long, trying to test the boundaries like sheep are so prone to do. Truth is, I was victim to the notion that I could serve both my faith and my pride.

It's an appealing idea.

It's also a lie; the missing piece.

An engineer can build an arched bridge of stone without a keystone, but it won't have any strength; apply a little pressure, and it will collapse. So, in reality, it's an illusion. That's what my faith was; for all its outward appearance, it was an illusion. The keystone of faith is absolute trust, and that's what I found was missing. Even though I knew and felt Jesus' love throughout all this, I didn't really trust Him; control was something I kept to myself. I never even considered it as something I needed to offer up to God. In fact, it was my lifeline, my Plan B – my Back-to-Egypt move in case God didn't work out. That fall-back was my idol: Special Forces and the pride and sense of belonging it gave me.

I wasn't finding my value in the Lord, but in my uniform and my medals; as much a part of me as my flesh.

It didn't take much insight to see myself in that sheep in the documentary. Spiritually, I'd rolled down a hillside and come to rest, on my back, on a tiny ledge. The slightest move in the wrong direction would send me to my death in the ravine, thousands of feet below. I was helpless to save myself; only the Shepherd could do that. The famous image of Jesus carrying a happy lamb back to the fold came to mind, but that was not my reality. He had to pick me up and carry me because I was utterly broken and confused, hanging onto life. And when He tried to stand me back up, it took a long time before I could stand on my own again, and be clear-minded enough to see outside myself. I was reminded of Matthew 18:12-14:

What do you think? If a man has a hundred sheep, and one of them has gone astray, does he not leave the ninety-nine on the mountains and go in search of the one that went astray? And if he finds it, truly, I say to you, he rejoices over it more than over the ninety-nine that never went astray. So it is not the will of my Father who is in heaven that one of these little ones should perish. – Jesus Christ

In my situation, as that sheep on the ledge, salvation required complete surrender. I had the choice to fight – which meant to fall – or trust completely in the Shepherd.

I'd done that before – years ago – but that was a different surrender then; maybe a partial one.

I had come to realize that the kind of surrender my Shepherd required was complete "go-limp-in-His-arms" surrender of control – of everything – without reservation, without resistance, without a Plan B. *That* I'd never done. Not only did I have to surrender, I had to put absolute trust in someone I couldn't even *see*!

So I did.

And so, after I'd retired from the Army and twenty-one years after I'd first considered Christian ministry, it finally dawned on me why God may not have allowed me to follow that path, at that time. Before that could happen, I had to get beyond the idea that I would find my value and validation as a member of the Special Forces. The lesson was hard come by, and I didn't really learn it until I retired. I didn't realize, at the time, that I wasn't just leaving the Army, I was leaving everything and everyone I'd known for over two decades. Suddenly the friends with whom I'd shared so much were gone, and with them the camaraderie. The danger was gone, as was the glory that came with confronting it.

Once again, after so long, I was alone – handcuffed to a past that wanted nothing to do with me. The whispers that rose from the stark silence of that loneliness were all-too familiar. "You're not worthy after all. It was all a show. You were just running from your own weakness and worthlessness, and now that you've stopped running . . ."

But the devil pushed his point a little too far. I realized that I was listening to lies: those the past told me, and those I told myself. I identified the Liar – the father of lies – and rebuked him and, just like that, the final piece of the puzzle – that of absolute trust in Christ, slipped into place. Finally, there was a keystone in my little bridge of faith. Now it could withstand any weight. Suddenly it seemed like a thousand doors opened at once and I was thrust into the center of public ministry.

That long-ago call to ministry hadn't been stillborn, after all, it was prophetic, and it had come to pass in the "fullness of time." I earned my MDiv and was ordained by my church as a minister to our large and thriving community of seniors where I served for over four years, some of whom are from *the greatest generation*. What an honor!

Having read this far, you know that getting to this point was a long journey through bitter trials and sufferings. Why was that necessary? I read in Scripture that "Christ became perfect through suffering." Since that principle applies to Christ, it makes sense that it applies to us, as well. In fact, Jesus Himself said, "In the world, you will have tribulation," fortunately, He followed that with, "but be of good cheer, for I have overcome the world."

His suffering is not an isolated example. In fact it's a recurring theme throughout the Bible, which is a chronicle of people suffering – independently and corporately – and it offers an explanation for that suffering: sin. If you haven't read the Bible, here's the plot: God created man in His own image – that is, He created them as beings with eternal souls – He created them to share, appreciate, and participate in all He had created, for all time. He created them for fellowship. He could, of course, have made them automatons who loved and worshiped Him because they had no choice, but that would be neither love nor worship. So He gave them free will – the ability to tell good from evil, and choose their path accordingly.

Mankind – represented in the story of Adam and Eve – chose evil (disobedience). That separated them from God, because He is not only good, He's perfect, and perfection and evil – like matter and anti-matter – can't co-exist.

Repeatedly, throughout the Old Testament, God called people to repent – that is ask His forgiveness – and return to Him. Some did, some didn't. Those who didn't paid the price – most often simply in the form of what happened as a consequence of their sinful actions, sometimes directly under God's judgment. But God didn't give up. Time and again He repeated His offer, sometimes rescuing them in miraculous ways from their enemies, or providing for them supernaturally. Sometimes, He just waited.

All the while, He was establishing the foundation of the

bridge by which all those lost people could return to Him. That bridge is His son, Jesus who would be the ultimate sacrifice for sin to all those who accepted Him as such. But first Jesus had to be proven perfect, and that perfection was achieved through suffering. Not only suffering on the cross; He suffered throughout the years of His ministry. Isaiah, the Old Testament prophet, foretold that He (the Messiah) would be a man "acquainted with suffering."

Those were days of political upheaval. Rome ruled the Mediterranean world, including Palestine (Israel) where Jesus lived. From birth, when Rome's puppet-king Herod tried to have him killed, Jesus was threatened by those to whom He was a threat. The Pharisees: religious traditionalists; the Sadducees: nominally-Jewish free-thinkers who occupied the highest strata in Jewish society (often the High Priest was among their number); the Sanhedrin: the high council or court of Jewish law, the Romans, the king, even His own family and one of His own disciples were arrayed against Him!

All were out to get Him, to catch Him in a lie or saying or doing something that could be interpreted as instigating revolt against the Roman Empire.

Throughout the few years of His ministry, He was constantly surrounded by people begging Him for a miracle, expecting Him to feed them. Some expected Him to raise an army and lead it in revolt against Rome.

He was always falling short of people's expectations.

He had no permanent home, but was constantly on the move, walking great distances in the heat and dust, the snow and cold, the rain and wind, sleeping outside. While His Spirit was that of God, His flesh was that of a man. No doubt His feet hurt, His back hurt, He felt exhaustion, and the burden of stress – after all, He knew His every footstep was bringing Him that much closer to a horrible death.

He was angry, sometimes, and frustrated – especially

with religious leaders and with His disciples – His heart broke for the people around Him, and for the Holy City of Jerusalem which, He prophesied, would be completely destroyed within just a few decades.

That prophecy was fulfilled in 70 A.D., when Rome razed the city to the ground.

And He had left everything, His job as a carpenter, His father's home in Nazareth where His mother, brothers and sisters lived, no doubt the friends among whom he had grown up and lived the first thirty years of His life.

He suffered, and in the midst of that suffering prayed that God would not make Him drink that final cup of suffering: death on the cross.

God did not remove that cup. And yet, the fruit of all that suffering was the offer of salvation to all the world! *All things work together for good to those who love the Lord and keep His commandments.* (Romans 8:28) *For God so loved the world, that He gave His only Son, that whoever believes in Him should not perish, but have everlasting life!"* (John 3:16)

We all suffer in countless ways, but we can expect that good will come of it in the end. Since this book is the story of my life, it's the story of my suffering, not to say mine was any worse or better than anyone else's, it's just my story, the one I know best, and from which I learned. Among those lessons was the answer to those perennial questions I addressed earlier.

Chapter Twenty-Three

So, what is this book of my life – my thoughts and experiences – about? What does it all mean and why did I feel it necessary to write it? Standing in places like the church Billy Graham was ordained in adds a sobering contrast to my life. Truthfully, when I began the project I had the grand notion that others would see their own lives in my suffering, and their healing in my healing.

Some months after I began to set words to the page, I came to realize that it was more self-reflection than anything. In the daily goals I set myself, there was a kind of lifeline, tugging me through the day. At one point, I looked back at my still-uncompleted manuscript – pages and pages of marked up paper – and understood that before I could make my story meaningful or helpful to others, I had to make sense of all that clutter and confusion myself.

I think that, details aside, my story is not uncommon as it relates to struggles, obstacles, and tragedies 'that human flesh is heir to.' Life is not just a pointless exercise in living for self and the satisfaction of our here and now, it's a quest for reunion with God our Father and Creator.

If nothing else, I hope and pray that in my story – and the healing I discovered in Jesus Christ – you will find encouragement for your own journey to healing.

Today

I live on the opposite side of the country from where I grew up. My parents and grandparents are gone. I still have relations on the west coast, but my real family, now, consists of my lovely wife Karen, whom I met in 1995 and married in '96, and our two college-aged children, our son Connor and daughter, Sydney. They have all suffered terribly - with me and because of me - as do countless others as they seek to understand and deal with the strangers who came home from war. It's all shrapnel.

While each of them have suffered in their own way, relative to their own perspective of suffering, none has ever known the kind of trials hundreds of thousands of soldiers experience, or the price that is paid to secure the freedoms they enjoy; a price paid not with flesh-and-blood alone but, sometimes, with sanity.

It could be said that I came to Christ through the suffering of the flesh. That may or may not be. In any event, it's probably not the path that will lead my children to Christ. They don't suffer from privation or constant danger.

How, then, will they be 'made perfect?'

I expect my PTSD, the remnants of a TBI, and the pain and tumult they and my wife had to live with as a result, will be the foundation of their own chronicle – and that, by

God's grace, good will come of it. Still, I write in hopes that, by knowing my story, they will understand me, what shaped me and made me the man I was, the man I am, and the man I hope to be. I make no excuses. I just offer an explanation.

I want them to see how Christ rescued me. How God's work on me was unique – as it is with each of us, because He knows us intimately, and loves only on condition that we accept that love.

Jesus had found me in a dark, godless, and lonely place. He'd picked me up – as many times as I slipped or fell – and transfused my spirit with the blood of His sacrifice until I was strong enough to stand. Then the Holy Spirit drew me to His side. I feel no inclination to wander. My greatest desire, now, is to take the love and forgiveness He pours on me *new every morning* (Lamentations 3:23), and extend it to others in His name.

Why did God work in my life the way He did?

Why does the blacksmith put iron through the fire? To refine it. To make it strong. To convert it from a lump of earth into something with purpose; something useful. Undoubtedly, The Lord – the master blacksmith – was using all these life experiences to prepare me to be useful.

Maybe He's doing that with you, too. To what end? Who knows? Does the hammer, or ax, or pot that emerges from the heat of the forge know what its ultimate use will be? No. Its maker only wants it to be ready when He's ready to use it.

In the case of those of us who believe, that readiness means reading the Bible, pondering its lessons, and applying them to our lives, day-to-day: keeping ourselves clear of what may entangle or tempt us: bathing our thoughts and deeds in prayer, and resting as securely as a babe in the arms of God having surrendered to His will.

In any event, I'm determined to do more, as a Christian,

than just mark time paddling in the kiddie pool of faith. I, too, am a man acquainted with suffering and I refuse to let its lessons be in vain. Every day I will intentionally venture further and further into the deep end of the pool, just as I did with my SCUBA training, conditioning myself – through Bible study and prayer, to me of greater service, to not only proclaim the Gospel, but to live it.

Northeast Florida, where I live today, is a place with a unique history. In 1563, long before the Pilgrims set foot on American shores, groups of Europeans, Catholics and Protestants, came here and promptly started killing each other. The name of a very popular inlet on the Intracoastal waterway is called Matanzas which, in Spanish means 'slaughter.'

When I walk those beaches, even when surrounded by the laughter, shouts, and general happy hub-bub of tourists, boaters, swimmers, and fishermen, I sense the anguish, the

hunger, fear, and desperation of those ancient explorers. Just a few minutes north, across the bridge that staples Anastasia island, where I live, to Saint Augustine – North America's oldest, continually-inhabited city – a huge cross dominates the landscape. In the early morning, it's shadow falls on the mainland, where there's no shortage of churches. Its evening shadow, though, doesn't quite reach across the inlet to the island. I'm not sure what that signifies, probably a poet or theologian could make something of it. In any case, there are only two churches on the island, one a Catholic church and Anastasia Church, where God called me to serve as a minister to the seniors until the fall of '20.

Perhaps the trials and suffering – the shaping and molding – we experience in life are allowed, or even ordained, so we can honor God the most when we get there.

I will say it again. *Perhaps the trials and suffering – the shaping and molding – we experience in life are allowed, or even ordained, so we can honor God the most when we get there.*

The word "Appreciate" also means to "recognize the full worth of something or to treasure, admire or respect something." Because I have seen so much of my own blood being poured out over the years, and have seen countless others bleed, I can recognize the full worth of Jesus's sacrifice on the cross and all the sacrifice and suffering that once took place on my adopted home shores.

Hebrews 13:8-16 says:

Jesus Christ is the same yesterday and today and forever. Do not be led away by diverse and strange teachings, for it is good for the heart to be strengthened by grace, not by foods, which have not benefited those devoted to them. We have an altar from which those who serve the tent have no right to eat. For the bodies of those animals whose blood is brought into the holy places by the high priest as a sacrifice for sin are burned outside the camp. So Jesus also suffered outside the gate in order to sanctify the people through his own blood.

Therefore let us go to him outside the camp and bear the reproach he endured. For here we have no lasting city, but we seek the city that is to come. Through him then let us continually offer up a sacrifice of praise to God, that is, the fruit of lips that acknowledge his name. Do not neglect to do good and to share what you have, for such sacrifices are pleasing to God.

So it seems the Lord constantly uses evil meant for harm, to glorify Himself. I believe the events in my life, past, present, and future, are all predestined and preordained. That doesn't mean God planned them – that would negate free will – He simply knew them beforehand, because He sees all time at a glance. He saw my life at a glance, and gave me the grace I needed to get through it.

Standing on the shore of Matanzas inlet, I sense the loss and privation of those long-gone warriors and explorers. It resonates with that abused little boy I carry around within me – the abandoned, hungry, and confused adolescent he became; the soldier seeking his father's approval by becoming a Green Beret; the wounded soldier/warrior alone on the tarmac in the middle of the night.

As a soldier, I had caused others a lot of pain and death. I had a lot to be forgiven for. It was in knowing I *was* forgiven that I learned the power of forgiveness, and the depth of love. That's a lesson you can't learn from books or lectures. It's also a lesson I regularly need to remind myself of.

Jesus was with me through my trials, always there at the very end of me.

As I write, I feel the Lord is calling me to a new ministry. What lies ahead? Well, finishing my doctoral thesis for now. But I also have my ideas pertaining to veterans ministry, but I'm going to be especially careful not to move too hastily. I'm going to wait, rest, and be still until I hear God's voice in my heart, and then – just like in parachute training – I'll jump!

One thing I know, I've learned empathy. I am sensitive when others are hurting. I can relate to them. I can minister to them, not just with platitudes, or even shared experience and suffering, but with the healing blood and love of Jesus. Everything I do will, I hope and pray, point others to the cross; anything less would be pointless. Most of all, I will be extravagant in distributing grace – of which I have received so much.

When all is said and done, it is God's grace and not all my striving, suffering, and sacrifice that has blessed me with the opportunity to serve. We all share in this grace – this emblem of God's love for us – our part is to simply accept it.

I also understand the unflinching, sacrificial love of Jesus by those who came before us, who were gripped by Jesus love for them, that they gave their lives for Him. Those people risked their lives crossing angry oceans, entering unknown, often extremely hostile environments, and enduring every imaginable privation and persecution to carry out Christ's command to 'go into all the world and spread the Gospel.'

When confronted by the option to recant their faith and live, they chose death. Like the martyrs who came before them throughout history, they chose obedience to Jesus. Just like blood being sprinkled over the altar, several thousand ounces of their thick, red fluid mixed and mingled in the waters surrounding this, Anastasia Island. The tides and currents carried the blood to the front, behind, to the left and right completing the purifying of this island whose name means "Resurrection."

"Search me, O God and know my heart; test me and know my anxious thoughts. See if there is any offensive way in me, and lead me in the way everlasting. (Psalm 139:23-24)." Even now, and maybe more so these days I ask Jesus if there is any hidden sin or temptation that has not been fully

revealed in me, that I might be cleansed and truly set free to daily serve Him. I want to enjoy Him and all He has for me and has purposed for my life. I desire to walk by His side, trusting Him to plant in my heart those seeds that will become my desires. Today, I need nothing more than Jesus' presence, which comforts me. I have finally learned the worth of this simple truth and these profound words. Receive these words also and understand them now more fully:

The Lord is my shepherd, I shall not be in want. He makes me lie down in green pastures, he leads me beside quiet waters, he restores my soul. He guides me in paths of righteousness for his name's sake. Even though I walk through the valley of the shadow of death, I will fear no evil, for you are with me; your rod and your staff, they comfort me. You prepare a table before me in the presence of my enemies. You anoint my head with oil; my cup overflows. Surely goodness and love will follow me all the days of my life, and I will dwell in the house of the Lord forever (Psalm 23).

I hope and pray that someday He will say, "Well done good and faithful servant." And I will say "I did not do that much, Lord." I want to hear Him say then, "When you saw me in need you helped me, you helped save and ministered to many." If we fully comprehended the great grace in these loving, undeserved rewards to come, what might our lives look like until that day arrives that grace may abound?

Entering my fourth decade as a believer and looking back over the rugged terrain of my journey, I'm able to clearly see God using the hardships and challenges I encountered along the way to guide me to the Truth, and draw me to Him and His love and acceptance – the prize my heart had been seeking all along.

Reading in Second Samuel recently, I could not help noticing what happened in David's life. In fact, I can relate. He seemed just like me in some ways. Always a little surprised, sometimes impressing God and sometimes getting in trouble for lack of thinking things through. David was a man after God's own heart. He loved having our Joyful God over him, but he spent many years being co-dependent with King Saul. Just like my own father-son relationship. Sometimes, I was the target and the reason my dad was angry with the world or himself, and at other times he was just upset that I seemed to have it easier. Jealously, I suppose. It was jealousy with Saul too. We sometimes forget that.

There was so much else that happened surrounding Saul and David, so much sorrow and bloodshed that might have been prevented if not for pride and envy. That was something Saul never confessed and it just became part of his nature, so ingrained, he never thought his jealousy and pride was the root of all his woes.

I expect we all have that in common with Saul; some weakness that has been so ingrained, so much a part of us, that we fail to see it for what it is; sin. Think how much better Saul's life would have been "if only."

Have you ever said that to yourself, "if only. . .?"

Several years ago, my dad passed on and is on the other side of eternity and I am still here to carry on, putting back together all the broken pieces and hopefully letting go of all the dysfunction. I'm certainly not going to deny that writing this book has been a kind of therapy to that end.

I have responsibilities to others and can't afford to drag the baggage and shadows of my past into every new day. Like David, my relationship with God is what I must make most important. He is my Rock. His blood covers my pride, jealousy, hate, and unforgiveness. He is my wealth. In Him, not in having been a Green Beret, is my self-esteem. I have value not because of what *I've* done or accomplished, but because of *who He is*, and what He – in His love for me – has done.

Johnny Cash said it best in one of his last recordings before his death in 2003: "You can have all my empires of piles of dirt." There was only one thing worth living for in the end. The One who was, and is, and is to come.

Reflecting again on my memorable trip to Israel those many years ago, it was easier then to visit the Temple Mount – also called Mount Mariah. Mike and I were actually allowed to go inside the Dome of the Rock. I'll never forget how pagan I felt. I wore shorts, and a tank top. The poor Muslim site manager looked at us with disdain, as if to say, "What are you thinking? Don't you know where you are standing?" He made us take off our shoes and wash our feet. We complied, but I still didn't understand why I was doing that.

Perhaps he didn't either. Like many things religious, it might have been tradition or ritual. However, who knows whether God – who uses everything for His glory – uses even the zealous Muslim overseers to preserve the sanctity of that spot, His Holy Ground, until His purpose for it is fulfilled? Little did I know, at the time, that even the Jews did not enter that place. Not because of the Muslims, but because it's where the Jewish Temple, the Ark of the Covenant itself – containing the tablets of the Ten Commandments and Aaron's rod – and the Holy of Holies, in which the Ark rested, once stood. In reverence, they treat the place as if the Temple stands there still, in anticipation that, one day, it will.

So, finally after washing our feet, we were allowed to go inside. It was somewhat dark but flood lighting was provided. There was a cement or tile-like floor and an area in the middle that was roped off, beyond which lay a huge smooth rock, rising in a gentle arch from one end to the other. This was the "foundation stone," the bedrock itself of where the original Temple had stood, possibly the very rock upon which Abraham prepared to sacrifice his son Isaac. One thing Jewish, Christian, and Muslim theologians agree upon, it was certainly part of the threshing floor that David bought as a place of sacrifice.

Of course, as the conquering warrior, King David could have simply seized the spot for himself, but we learn in Samuel's account that, though its owner, Augraus, offered it to him for nothing – David insisted: "No, but I will buy it from you for a price. I will not offer burnt offerings to the Lord my God that cost me nothing!"

Worshiping and loving our Heavenly Father will cost us something. He said it would. He said we would suffer, be persecuted, even be hated for His namesake. That's not comfortable, but we weren't put here for comfort. It's in embracing this kind of discomfort that we begin to cast aside the chains that bind our testimony. But there must be a desire and willingness to surrender all, not a forced compliance to do so.

Curiously, when, in obedience to His command, we

physically go and do, and it costs us something, a physical, spiritual transformation takes place. Our heart comes out of hiding – we become more empathetic and sympathetic – and Christ's Holy Spirit within us is invigorated and emboldened. It's a beautiful illustration of the fruit of our devotion to Him, our Creator.

King David surrendered willingly without regret, making his worship authentic and beautiful.

Today, with the exception of the Dome of the Rock, the Temple Mount stands barren. In the area that would, in Jesus' day, have been the outer precincts of the Temple, it's easy to picture – were the dome removed – an entire new Temple being lowered from the sky and set down perfectly upon its foundation without disturbing a thing.

That's what Scripture seems to say will happen one day.

There may be thousands of reasons why God chose mount Mariah and the Temple Mount as a place of holiness on earth. But He possibly chose a threshing floor as a symbol because it is a place of work and separation. In order to separate the wheat from the chaff, one ingredient is very necessary. It must have a steady wind. Thrown up towards heaven, the chaff from the wheat blows away, carried by the wind, and the wheat – food for a nation – falls back to the threshing floor. Metaphorically, we are all brought to the threshing floor. God uses the circumstances, challenges, trials, tribulations, and joys of life to separate us from our sin nature just as the chaff is separated from the wheat. He calls us to offer up to Him, in worship, who we are, to let His Holy wind carry away all that does not belong in us, that keeps us from Him.

It seems, then, that we all have our own inner David and Saul. We all deal with pain, whether it comes from without – as with the abuse I experienced at my father's hand – or within, meaning poor decisions and their consequences. Covetousness, pride, envy, these things sneak up on us like they did with Saul and King David. Hopefully we feel the weight of God's conviction and seek forgiveness, as David did. That conviction brings us to our greatest act of courage: falling on our knees in front of everybody in "David-like" humility, not being too proud to bring our sacrifice – ourselves – to the threshing floor.

As we've seen, Abraham went to the top of that uninhabited mountain long before David did. Several hundred years later, during the Jebusite days, Mount Mariah was terraced, several levels of wheat and barley grew on the slopes leading up.

All of these crops were destined for the threshing floor on the top of the mountain. Everything in various stages of growth on those terraces was tended to, watered, and harvested. Tufts of wheat and barley that had fallen from the bundles of grain as they were carried along the trails leading to the top lay un-sifted, unwinnowed, still sheathed in their chaff. But up on the mountain, the grain that made it was being thrown into the air where the wind blew the chaff away, and the kernels fell to earth – to what would one day be the floor of the Holy of Holies – perfect and whole, ready to be used: to feed and strengthen.

But some will one day undoubtedly say, "If only I'd . . . "

I pray my story has inspired you, helped you, spoken to you. I hope your life comes full circle to living out the simple truth that, in fact, all roads eventually lead to God. One way or another we will meet our Creator for better or worse. Live each day as if it's the day for that glorious reunion – without fear. It will turn all your yesterdays into non-regrets and will bring glory to our Father who is more than worthy.

He never wastes what we have gone through but will, ultimately, put it all to good use. And our tomorrows? They can be used to bring Himself additional moments of glory by you, His willing and available vessel. All of our lives and the experiences we have faced, if offered up joyfully, will be used to make us the very best persons for Him. We will finally see that all our empires were simply piles of dirt compared to having a friend in our Father and Creator. The Lord did not lose anything nor did He regret His choice to atone for us. We are worth the price especially because of all our accumulated shrapnel.

Chapter Twenty-Four

I'd like to leave you with a sermon I delivered at my church a few years ago. I think it sums up much of what needs to be said here. I am glad I went through all that I have if it brings me, and you, to a better place with our God. May the Lord bless you and keep you forever and ever. In Christ Jesus our Lord, I pray. Amen.

"This is Memorial Day weekend and we want to acknowledge all those who made the ultimate sacrifice. Jesus made another kind of ultimate sacrifice. His is the one that matters on an eternal level. We live forever because of His atonement made for us.

Today I'd like to speak about soldiers in the Bible. In thinking and praying about this message, what was brought to my mind was the encounter between the Roman Centurion and Jesus. Let's stand in honor of the reading of God's word.

Matthew 8:5-10

"When he had entered Capernaum, a centurion came forward to him, appealing to him, "Lord, my servant is lying paralyzed at home, suffering terribly." And he said to him, "I will come and heal him." But the centurion replied, "Lord, I am not worthy to have you come under my roof, but only say the word, and my servant will be healed. For I too am a man under authority, with soldiers under me. And I say to one, 'Go,' and he goes, and to another, 'Come,' and he comes, and to my servant, 'Do this,' and he does it." When Jesus heard this, he marveled and said to those who followed him, "Truly, I tell you, with no one in Israel have I found such faith." (Matthew 8:5-10).

Summarizing what we know is happening here, we see the following: In Jesus' day a Roman centurion would have been equivalent to a captain in today's army. He would have had a hundred men under his command. He was an officer who was promoted through the ranks by showing extraordinary bravery and leadership in battle and was committed to serve for a twenty-year period. He would not have been allowed marriage because of his duty assignments, but would have had a servant to assist him. He would have no family especially for the years of his deployments to Palestine. He only needed to say things once though. He was a commander with great authority.

I'm going to draw this imaginary line across the stage in front of you and ask that you remember it. I will come back to it later.

So in the story, Jesus was amazed at the Centurion's faith. Or you could say, his faith amazed Jesus. Either way, I like the way it is translated in another popular version. It says, "Jesus turned him towards the crowd" and showed him to them, announcing the stunning faith he witnessed. The man was a pagan, a gentile, a heathen, and Jesus was telling the chosen people of God, the Jews, that a gentile had shown more faith than any of them. To be clear Jesus was not talking about the prophets and leaders of old, but those in His own lifetime.

The word I find myself focusing on is "marveled" or "amazed." I mean, that is serious language that is being used here. It literally means Jesus was filled with wonder or astonishment and/or being greatly surprised. Think about that. What would it take for you to be "greatly surprised" or "astonished?" And we're talking about Jesus here. This is saying a lot. If He was "greatly" surprised, that means the opposite words came out of the centurion's mouth than Jesus ever expected.

I imagine this intimidating authority figure inching his way through the crowd in order to come close enough for Jesus to hear him say, whispering, "Lord, my servant is lying paralyzed at home, suffering terribly." Jesus says, "I will come heal him." But this is when the man says, "Say the word, I too am a man under authority..." This is where Jesus turns and looks at him with "astonishment."

So the point I am making is that a soldier, by Jesus's

own admission, was shown to demonstrate the greatest faith to Jesus! And the only compliment Jesus ever gave, as written in the New Testament, was to this soldier.

I want you to notice a pattern; the most pivotal moments accomplished in Jesus' life. The greatest faith He had ever seen was from a soldier. God used dependable soldiers. He could count on them to aid in condemning Him; to correctly confine Him; to professionally escort Him; to follow their orders, without question, to give Him lashings, to crucify Him without delay and by the book. They were honored to touch Him last, still alive, to take His clothing, to pierce Him, to provide Him a last drink, probably referred to by "forgive them Father, for they know not what they do." They were of the last to see Him in the tomb, to guard His tomb, to witness His resurrection, to officially report that He was gone, to go looking for Him, and to record it in record. And was it not a soldier who first recognized upon Jesus death, that "Surely this is the Son of God?" And the first gentile or non-Jew to ever be baptized in Jesus name was Cornelius the Centurion.

If I do not tell my story then it just remains a private set of memories. If I, no matter how painful and vulnerable it makes me feel, share it, God can heal others and help us learn from them for the future, maybe saving lives.

Pride was keeping me from ever telling my story. But then I thought about the D-Day footage we have all seen over and over again. You know the one I'm talking about. It is a moment captured in black and white of men running up the Normandy beach and a soldier appears to get shot and falls to the ground in a heap. In that moment of war, his ultimate sacrifice was caught on camera.

Thanks to this footage, we do not conduct warfare like this anymore. How many countless lives has God saved showing this scene? I tried to find out his name, but it seems to be lost to the ages. He was just another casualty.

His life was not given in vain though, and we will not forget him or all the others who gave their lives that day.

Now I will tell you briefly about one of my own Normandy Beach moments. I was duty bound to learn loyalty and dependability.

I learned and grew and became a good, reliable soldier. Years later after joining the Army Special Forces, I found myself on my first combat deployment.

And here I want to go back to what I did when I drew across the stage earlier..

Back to the line in the sand I first spoke of. In February of 1823, the air was cool. For 13 days the 283 some odd defenders of the Alamo were under siege by 6000 of the Mexican Army. On March 5, there was a lull in the bombardment. The enemy was getting ready to launch his final assault on the now vulnerable and weakened fort.

Lieutenant Colonel William Travis, commander of the Fort, assembled the men. A choice had to be made and some decisions made. In a word, he said to the weary men standing before him, "No one else is coming to help, and we cannot keep the enemy out any longer. They are coming into this fort. I am going to stay here and fight and in a few hours, maybe less, I will be dead. I will not lie to you. If you stay here you will be killed with me. I am not ordering any man, but any man who is willing, knowing he is going to die this day fighting the enemy coming over these walls, I am asking you to fight with me."

Colonel Travis then took out his sword and drew a line from one end of the men to the other. Once complete, he came back to the center on one side of the line, and with a pause and pained look on his face, said "As I see it, you have three choices. You can surrender – "Never!" someone shouted. You can escape – "Ain't running!" another said. Or you can cross this line and die with me fighting for this cause – and this choice was met with silence. Then it happened. One by one, all but one crossed the line that day. They all perished fighting to defend the Alamo, but they also knew they would not die in vain – that Texas would be victorious.

I've often wondered about this piece of history. What would that moment be like to be staking the rest of my life on that decision? But mostly, I wonder why Colonel Travis drew a line in the sand. Why didn't he just ask for a decision? Or have people raise their hands? I think I know the answer. You see, it was not just that precise moment he was concerned about. He was thinking about all the harrowing moments he knew were going to take place after that decision had been made. He knew that when things got really bad, or doubt and fear filled their minds and sapped their will, they would need a physical, visible reminder of the point at which they willingly stepped across that line.

I can just see one of those tense moments; at one moment feeling all alone on their stretch of wall, trying to repel the enemy, but realizing that – despite their best efforts – the enemy is coming over. Their first impulse would be to save themselves. But, if they took the time, a quick glance to the left and right would reveal his fellow defenders still standing their ground, focused on their own battle. From them, he would draw the strength to stand.

Those of us who call ourselves Christian – after all, we were baptized and went to Sunday School or church, maybe joined a youth group, or went to Christian camp – should ask ourselves if we believe, really believe, to the point of surrender. Or do we, like an alarming majority, treat Jesus like an accessory rather than the centerpiece and focus of our life?

The question is, where do we stand in relationship to Christ? The answer is, we're either all in, or we're not in.

This is the part where I remind you of that line I drew in front of you. This is the part where you expect me to ask you to come forward and cross that line. Many of you will be greatly relieved to find that that's not my plan. Why? Because all of you stepped over that line, figuratively, the moment you accepted Christ as your Savior! Not only your Savior, but Lord of your life!

I want this line to serve only as a visual reminder of your position on the wall, together with your co-defenders. So when we see a line, I pray it reminds us that we stand together, against a common foe.

So what does God want for you? Besides believing and accepting Him, He wants to be marveled and amazed by your faith.

Do you think that Christ marvels at your faith – that He finds it amazing? Do you live it out in the assurance of victory? Do you carry yourself as a victor, in the knowledge that you are an heir of God Almighty, or as a victim? Are you set apart for holy purposes and membership in the holy priesthood? Or do you – like so many – just drift through life in the vague hope that you are saved?

That's not victorious living; it's living like you just couldn't quite bring yourself to cross that line.

So picture that same line behind you now. It is at the back of the room. The only thing in front of you is God's throne and altar. You are standing in His presence in Christ Jesus. We are one Body of believers, which cannot stand any closer to Him than we are right now. And getting that close, like the centurion, knowing if he could just get close enough for Him to hear, he could whisper, "Lord, say the word and it will be done." So Jesus could say, "Go: let it be done for you as you have believed." As you have believed!!

For myself, I was scared to do any of it. I did not want to get in that vehicle; I did not want to go to war; I did not want to commit to anything or anyone; I did not want to make a mistake; I did not want to die jumping out of perfectly good airplanes, but I did it. And, at one time, I did not want to be a member of a church; and I did not want to be counted on to minister; and I did not want to stand in front of 950 people and be vulnerable to criticism and disappointment, but I am doing that too. And I do it because I know the Lord meets me and blesses every consecrated step I take for having already stepped over that line of victory.

I don't know that I have ever amazed Jesus myself. But looking back, I am pretty amazed at what I was willing to do because of Him being in my life."

That was the end of the sermon.

A Final Thought

I want to convey the following. Life can hurt. It can be confusing. It can be scary and difficult. From being abused as a child, to having a lisp, to becoming a Green Beret, then a shy believer, to finally a man consumed by his Savior and Lord, it seems I have been traveling up Mount Mariah hill like so many before me. In the end, all my suffering had worked good in me. Whether I always knew it or not, I had been flowing up to the perfect Mountain of the Lord – to that Holy threshing floor that Jesus bought for me.

How can one flow uphill though?

"It shall come to pass in the latter days that the mountain of the house of the LORD shall be established as the highest of the mountains, and shall be lifted up above the hills; and all the nations shall flow to it. (Isaiah 2:2)." As the Word says, *"What is impossible with man is possible with God."*

Most often we only learn God's plan in retrospect. I was designed by Him to do "good works." (Ephesian 2:10). Satan always means to do harm and thwart God's plans. He has no power to win, though, but he just keeps trying, probably all the more desperate because he knows – or at least suspects – his ultimate fate, and that there's no escape from it.

You remember the account of Joseph who was sold into slavery by his brothers? In Genesis 50:20, he says: "You intended to harm me, but God intended it for good to accomplish what is now being done, the saving of many lives." This declaration is thought by many to prefigure Christ, about whom the same thing can be said.

I have suffered and I have all but died. I have lost my way and I have found my way. I have taken much and been given much, I have lost much and I have gained much. At the end of it all, I am certain of only one thing; God's victory in me required my defeat. Today I look back and see that I was never alone; my best friend and helper was always within reach - but I had to do the reaching too, and finally I did. And when I did, I discovered my real, eternal value as a son, brother, husband, father, soldier, Christian and mentor.

Christ raised me from the ashes of myself, turned my scars and shrapnel to testimony, and my suffering to a victory banner. It's been worth the cost.

Page 95, PACE COUNT: Distance traveled, or pace count, had to be precise, this is called Pace Count. You can buy a pace count keeper or make them. It is usually a piece of green parachute chord that you have tied individual sliding knots or affixing tight fitting beads to. It can have an upper portion of five knots separated by a lower section of ten knots. For each estimated one hundred meters walked (which for me, with a pack on, walking very fast with long strides, a hundred meters usually was seventy-eight steps counted every other left step). I would then pull down one knot separating it from the rest. After ten knots were pulled down, that would account for one thousand meters walked, so I would pull down one of the top five knots which would represent one km or kilometer, better known as a "Klick".

Page 106, THE BALLAD OF THE GREEN BERETS - Billboard's Song of the Year in 1966, was written by Staff Sergeant Barry Sadler and Robin Moore.

Page 119, Mr. Sandman, written by Pat Ballard - BMI

Page 121, CROSS-LOADED: This simply means everyone got the same amount. For example, if I have 20 cases of belts of ammunition but only have 12 guys, all the cases get broken down and distributed evenly among the twelve guys. There might be 5 belts of ammo in one case. Everyone gets the same amount and if we lose someone, our mission can continue.

Page 126, FINNING: For the most part, it is what it sounds like. However, in Combat Diving (frogman diving) it is the function of traveling very far and very fast underwater by way of high volume, wide sweeping scissor kicks, over and over. It is the natural way one would want to use flippers under water but done at extreme pace and efficiency, maximizing the fins surface area not unlike a very strong and efficient dolphin or another ocean mammal.

Page 144: Pulling security means you move to a location that *needs essential weapons fire cover and capability for a designated sector of enemy ground. Each able soldier finds a good fighting position where a wall of security can be mounted with cross-fire capability.*

Page 151, LARYNGOSCOPE: This is a metal apparatus used to force open a patient's airway, so they can insert the breathing tube down someone's throat.

Page 153, MASTER SERGEANT KEVIN MOREHEAD: My teammate for many years who became the Team Sergeant, E-8, for our ODA. He and one other SF soldier from another ODA were killed during the initial phase of assaulting a compound outside of Baghdad, in Al Ramadi. Kevin, who was the Team Sergeant, elected to go over the wall first and secure the courtyard and was ambushed. A grenade was thrown and then machine-gun fire was sprayed. Bullets ruptured his spleen and he died after being dragged out of the courtyard. The HVTs, or High Value Targets, dangerous and deadly terrorists, were all ultimately captured and or killed. Kevin received a posthumous Silver Star for his actions.

Page 167, FRIENDLY FIRE: QUESTION: It's believed the radio had reset the coordinates when the batteries were changed out. (they needed to be manually re-imputed or the Bombers would think the coordinates it was given were where they wanted the bombs dropped). My friend Dan put the radio in the hands of an Air Forces TAC-P sergeant while he ran back to another location briefly. Tactical Air Controller-Provider is what that stands for. They usually go with us so they can talk to the Air Force better. This obviously was not a good example of this. (Not for the book), but thought I would add, my other friend Mike was carrying two 5 gallon cans of diesel fuel when the bomb was dropped. He lost his right arm and his left was hanging on by only a few muscles. He was propped up against a wall, his body drenched in diesel fuel while he waited over 8 hours to be medevaced out. He made a grown Delta Force soldier cry his eyes out over seeing his desperate condition. Mike had to ask the man to pull down his pants and flush him with water to stop the diesel from eating and burning away his skin.

Page 172: This refers to our patrol base perimeter gates that were manned 24 hours a day. The last friendly face I saw was ironically some low paid Iraqi soldiers whom I never met. They were all just strangers and nameless faces. I was leaving the comfort and safety of them, who, otherwise, I would not care to know. The last friendly faces I would see were really just shadowy silhouettes.

Page 174-175, LIEUTENANT ALI: The mission of the US Military was to support Iraqi soldiers. It was their job to lead missions, not ours. We always try to help them do that. Ali led the patrol, but soon he lost confidence in his land navigation abilities. He was getting lost. My vehicle pulled in front of his, and I led the rest of the way to our objective. Once we got back onto the road not too far from the village, Ali took back the lead since he could now easily find his way. When we got near the village, the ambush started. I made my vehicle go around his, so he could be protected by our front armor (bullets were coming from our front as well). But usually, the best way out of an ambush is to rush through, to keep going and not stop. Ali was slowing and I hoped we could get the patrol quickly through. Once over the far side of the bridge, we were met with much more intense fire. No one was following us across the bridge. I finally turned us around and wanted Ali to follow us, so we could fight from further back. He did not or could not follow. I did not initially know he did not follow us. I then saw that I needed to get "much" of the rest of the Iraqi patrol doing something. They were not moving and receiving a lot of enemy fire. In other words, I had to withdraw another 100 meters further away the bridge back towards the village to help them. Once I (meaning my Command vehicle) got them moving and clearing the village, I could see elements of the patrol (both US and Iraqi) had *kept slowly moving forward to the bridge, over the bridge, different parts of the wadi, and attempting to cross their vehicles across it. The bridge was partially blocked by vehicles staying uncommitted. Most of the SF vehicles however were across the bridge and past Ali's vehicle and parked, returning fire in the flat desert, semi- circled in front of the bridge with Ali behind them. I raced back to cross the bridge to join them. We had to squeeze around vehicles that were partially blocking the bridge. It was more like a two lane bridge. Once we did this, others started clearing the bridge and getting across.*

Page 193 - Explosive Ordnance Disposal: These teams specialize in explosives. They travel to your location or operate within a certain sector and conduct an array of explosives disposal activities (usually blowing things up to get rid of other explosives, bombs, weapons, suspicious vehicles, bags, etc.) They also conduct investigations and give expert analysis.

Page 194 - Permissive, Semi-Permissive Environments: These are danger or threat zones as the military defines them. They are either friendly (permissive), semi-friendly or safe (semi-permissive), meaning you must be cautious, usually need to be armed knowing there are those that wish to do you harm and are actively seeking to do so, and then there is (non-permissive), meaning every attempt to operate in said environment will be perceived as a hostile threat and to expect much resistance and or violent opposition to your presence.

Page- 259 *Karen.

I met my beautiful wife *Karen* in the Fall of 1995. I had just arrived back on active duty at Fort Campbell, Kentucky when a barracks friend of mine, David, invited me out for the evening. He wanted to go meet a friend at a restaurant who happened to invite a friend of her own. When we got to the restaurant he started talking to his friend, which left Karen and me to get acquainted. It was not long before both of us realized we had a lot in common and enjoyed each other's company. We started dating but it was not long before my new Army job took me away for regular periods of time.

That first meeting took place in early November and by January I was deployed to Haiti. In February I was deployed to Fort Bragg, North Carolina for Special Forces Pre-SCUBA training. I returned to Fort Campbell briefly, then was off to Pakistan by April to train with the Pakistani Special Forces. In June, I was at Key West attending the Special Forces Underwater Operations school and did not get back home until July. In August, I was back in Pakistan training with the Pakistani Special Forces. When I returned in September, someone recommended that I go to Ranger School for another two plus months.

Instead, with so little time together, we took advantage of what little time we had before I was to leave again. I was thirty and she thirty-two respectively. It was amazing we got to know each other at all with the pace of training I was involved in!

Nevertheless, on October 14th we drove to Gatlinburg, Tennessee—where we had already contacted a retired minister who supplemented his income by officiating at weddings and there, in front of the fireplace in the house he and his wife shared, on a beautiful autumn day, almost a year after we met, we exchanged vows. It was a simple ceremony and that seemed just fine. A few months later we had a 'formal' wedding in California with all our family and friends. It was Christmas time, so we scheduled the ceremony to be held on 28 December 1996.

Soon after we got back, we bought a little A-frame home out in the country and, before we knew it, were expecting our first child to arrive. I was often deployed for weeks and months at a time and, during one such deployment our son Conner was born. Two years later our daughter Sydney arrived.

I cannot say enough about how wonderful Karen has been as both wife and mother, and that I love her. I was gone for more than half the children's lives and, during that time—as is true of so many military wives—she had to be both mother and father to the kids. They are fortunate to have grown up with her constant care and attention.

We raised the kids for four years in Clarksville, Tennessee, just outside Fort Campbell, and then for another three years in Key West, Florida where I was temporarily assigned as a Dive Instructor. Another nine years were spent back in Clarksville and Fort Campbell. Upon my retirement in 2013, we moved to Saint Augustine, Florida where both Conner and Sydney finished high school and went to college.

Conner Graduated with honors from high school and attained the rank of Eagle Scout in the Boy Scouts of America. He went on to attend Florida State University, graduating *summa cum laude* in May of 2015.

He finished in three years and elected to stay for a fourth year to earn a second bachelor's degree, ultimately graduating with honors in Political Science and a degree in International Relations. He was heavily involved in the World Affairs program, traveling and competing in debates all across the country, and even attended a few conferences in Croatia and Greece.

After college and serving for a year in AmeriCorps in Chicago as a disaster, aid, and response specialist, he has subsequently begun work with The American Red Cross as a case manager. His aspirations lie in pursuing service-oriented positions where he hopes to bring positive change and relief to suffering people everywhere.

Sydney, also an honor student, went on to graduate *cum laude* from the University of North Florida, also in three years. Obtaining a degree in Social Work, and participating in Social Work internships, she graduated in May 2020 at the tender age of twenty. During her time in college she also worked as a nursery school teacher and assistant at a local church. Upon her return from UNF, she was soon recommended for the position of teacher's assistant at the prestigious Florida School for the Deaf and Blind, in St. Augustine. She loves serving and working with the students, and aspires to help teach as much as possible.

Both Conner and Sydney are compassionate and sensitive to the needs of others. They do not help people because they feel pressured or compelled to do so, they do it because their desire is to positively influence other people's lives. They're both smart, focused and, if I may say so, are true blessings to the world. We could not ask for better children.

I wish I could take credit for influencing their devotion, but much of their character was developed by their first-hand familiarity with the many aspects of suffering to which people — soldiers and civilians alike — are routinely exposed during war and military conflict. They suffered themselves, because of me, and that makes them empathetic to the suffering of others.

Saving the best for last, Karen—a women full of grace—has been battered by life's difficult circumstances. Embracing her Scott-Irish heritage, she is not reticent about expressing her opinions, which no one knows better than I. However, love is at the root of her motivation, as is the intensity and determination she brings to life.

That passion is not always easily contained.

At thirty-two, she joined the Air Force and became a Flight Medical Technician for the Tennessee Air National Guard. She flew as a crew member on C-130 aircraft, the Air Force equivalent of a paramedic. The mission of the C-130s was, and is, to treat casualties from the battlefield and transport them to safety for additional medical support. She managed to do this while raising two amazing children, and making it seem surprisingly easy.

Today, Karen keeps providing the adhesive that holds the family and the home together, while also volunteering time to a local veteran's organization that helps our community by growing plants and flowers.

As I write this, I am reminded that Karen — my gal from Savannah — and I are in our third decade of marriage. I am so thankful for her. By God's design, she is a big reason why I have been able to achieve some things and our children turned out so well.

I hope these words further help acknowledge the love and appreciation I have for her. One day, God willing, she and I will see, on the other side of this life, just how much she was used to make our family what it is today. God bless my precious fellow-traveler, this wonderful wife of mine.

ACKNOWLEDGEMENTS

I would like to take this opportunity to thank David Crossman who, together with Danielle Jordan and Jane Morar, edited this book from the material I provided and without whom I could not have hoped to finish it. I would also like to acknowledge Nancy Quatrano who did much to help launch my first work upon which this book is based. They helped bring my words to life and gave structure and meaning to my often fragmented thoughts. The patience and kindness they have shown me in order to complete this autobiographical work has been beyond gracious.

Also, ironically, no thanks to the COVID pandemic of 2020- and beyond, though it caused many tragedies, it also provided me the time and opportunity to complete this testimony of hope I've been working on for so long; what was meant to harm, will, I pray, ultimately be used for good.

Finally, to all the brothers and sisters in arms I lost in Iraq and Afghanistan, in fact, from all our conflicts, thank you for your sacrifice and the continued inspiration you provide for us all. *De Oppresso Liber.*